Date: 7/29/20

BIO HECKMAN
Heckman, Meg,
Political godmother : Nackey
Scripps Loeb and the

POLITICAL GODMOTHER

POLITICAL GODMOTHER

NACKEY SCRIPPS LOEB and the NEWSPAPER THAT SHOOK the REPUBLICAN PARTY

MEG HECKMAN

POTOMAC BOOKS   An imprint of the University of Nebraska Press

Library of Congress
Cataloging-in-Publication Data
Names: Heckman, Meg, author.
Title: Political godmother: Nackey Scripps
Loeb and the newspaper that shook the
Republican Party / Meg Heckman.
Description: Lincoln: Potomac Books, an
imprint of the University of Nebraska
Press, 2020. | Includes bibliographical
references and index.
Identifiers: LCCN 2019034384
ISBN 9781640121935 (hardback)
ISBN 9781640123342 (epub)
ISBN 9781640123359 (mobi)
ISBN 9781640123366 (pdf)
Subjects: LCSH: Loeb, Nackey Scripps,
1924–2000. | Publishers and publishing—
New Hampshire—Biography. | Newspaper
editors—New Hampshire—Biography. |
Manchester union leader.
Classification: LCC PN4874.L587 H44 2020 |
DDC 070.92 [B]—dc23
LC record available at
https://lccn.loc.gov/2019034384

Set in Chaparral Pro by Laura Buis.
Designed by L. Auten.

For Brian. With you, it's all possible.

Contents

Illustrations

Acknowledgments

Writing this book felt a lot like running a marathon—a long, hard, and entirely worthwhile process made easier by a crowd of people offering logistical support and encouragement. Many of my colleagues at Northeastern University's School of Journalism provided crucial assistance. I'm especially indebted to Laurel Leff and Dan Kennedy for their thorough, thoughtful, and blazingly quick editing of my initial manuscript. This book is better because of their efforts. I also received excellent feedback from Jonathan Kaufman and John Wihbey. When I got lost in the weeds of twentieth-century political history, Chuck Fountain and Alan Schroeder pointed me in the right direction. Susan Conover made the business side of book writing a lot easier by helping me hire research assistants and process expense reports from trips to multiple archives. My wonderful students cheered me on, commiserated about deadlines, and on a day when I was feeling especially distracted, shooed me back into my office to finish a chapter. And research assistants Edie Allard, Catherine McGloin, Brilee Weaver, and Eileen O'Grady kept the archival work moving along.

I also received vital support—both financial and technical—from Northeastern's NULab for Texts, Maps, and Networks. A seed grant the lab awarded me in the fall of 2017 allowed me to aggregate, digitize, and analyze all of Nackey Loeb's editorials using basic digital humanities techniques. The results of that work helped me pierce through a persistent (and inaccurate) narrative that Nackey had been a passive publisher who wasn't very much involved in national politics. What

I discovered during that process helped me focus my reporting, ask better questions, and build the backbone of this book.

I had help outside of Northeastern too. Early readers—especially Jane Harrigan and Clay Wirestone—made the first stages of this project feel less daunting. My friends and family tolerated my frequent travel, the many long hours I spent in my office, and other assorted eccentricities that come with writing a book. They sent encouraging text messages, dragged me outside, and appeared on my doorstep with snacks. I am indebted to you all.

Introduction

Nackey Scripps Loeb smiled as the phone calls came into a makeshift TV studio in downtown Manchester, New Hampshire. The state's 1988 presidential primary was a few days away, and she was appearing live on C-SPAN to discuss what role her unusual—and unusually influential—local newspaper might play in the outcome of the race. The *Union Leader* is as much a part of the Granite State's political lore as town hall meetings, towering snow banks, and candidates hustling for votes in diners and on factory floors. But as host Bruce Collins was discovering, Nackey's appeal transcended both the election cycle and geography. Many of the callers that day were loyal out-of-state subscribers who received their papers by mail and were thrilled at the chance to speak to Nackey.

"You have many admirers here in the South," said a man from Louisiana. "We appreciate your editorial view." Someone from North Carolina wished the Union Leader Corporation would buy the newspaper in Asheville and make it less liberal. Other callers worried about communism, complained about U.S. policy toward South Africa, and lamented that the Iran-Contra scandal might harm President Reagan's legacy—all flash points in the conservative movement at the time. One man from Virginia, part of Nackey's vast and devoted network of letter writers, wanted to know if she'd received his latest submission. She had, and she thanked him for all the mail.

"I did not pay all these people to call in," Nackey said, grinning. "It sounds as though there are a lot of fans out there, and I appreciate it."

The out-of-state calls continued, and Collins looked surprised.

"Do you think of yourself as a national figure?" he asked.

"I never spend too much time wondering about what I think about myself," Nackey replied. "I take what I believe in very seriously. I take what we are doing here at the paper very seriously, but fortunately I've never taken *myself* all that seriously."[1]

In reality, Nackey was very much a national figure by 1988. As she gamely chatted up C-SPAN viewers on that chilly February day, she was on the cusp of the most public phase of her activism, one that would contribute to the rightward reshuffling of the Republican Party during the final years of the twentieth century. She accomplished this by building a loyal, sprawling audience and leveraging it to back Patrick Buchanan's conservative challenge to incumbent President George H. W. Bush in the 1992 GOP primary. She supported Buchanan again in the 1996 election. When he won New Hampshire that year, he used part of his victory speech to declare her his "political godmother."[2] Buchanan, of course, never became president. But his populist, isolationist rhetoric connected with a segment of the electorate that remains influential in the modern political landscape.

The endurance and evolution of the GOP's right wing is the result of many complex, long-simmering issues and ideologies, but Nackey Scripps Loeb was an important player—a fact that is largely absent from accounts of presidential politics and New Hampshire's first-in-the-nation primary. The *Union Leader* itself gets plenty of attention, but the stories are almost always focused on Nackey's husband, William Loeb. Every four years, journalists from around the world rehash how he used hyperbolic, hyper-conservative front-page editorials to influence elections from the time he bought his first Granite State newspaper in the mid-1940s until his death in 1981. He wasn't always a kingmaker, but he drove the political narrative in a way that continues to shape civic life in New Hampshire today. He was a fascinating figure—gun-toting, litigious, a little eccentric, and entirely unafraid to speak his mind—but an obsession with his outlandish legacy has left Nackey and her work in the 1980s and 1990s largely overlooked.

For instance, in January of 2000 the *New York Post* dispatched columnist Steve Dunleavy to Manchester, where the *Union Leader* had just endorsed the billionaire longshot candidate Steve Forbes. In a story headlined "Voice from the Grave Calls Out for Forbes," Dunleavy declared, "The ghost of old Bill Loeb can still pack a killer punch."[3] Dunleavy was right about a deceased Loeb influencing the endorsement, but he focused on the wrong one. It was Nackey who, in the final months of her life, consulted with her colleagues about backing Forbes. She'd led the paper for nearly twenty years and had died just a few weeks before Dunleavy came to New Hampshire, but his column never mentions her name. More recently, the *Washington Post* had to correct a 2016 article that misattributed some of Nackey's writing during the 1988 primary to her late husband.[4] These stories and many others contribute to a common and inaccurate narrative in which Nackey is marginalized, underestimated, or omitted. The accounts are so pervasive that it's tempting to imagine her as a disengaged manager, or perhaps as a woman who was interesting only because of the husband she chose. Those assumptions are wrong, and this book will show why.

Nackey Scripps Loeb was a powerful newspaperwoman in her own right and, during the second half of the twentieth century, an influential voice within the conservative movement. Hers is a story of reinvention, both political and personal. She was born into the wealthy Scripps publishing family, the granddaughter and daughter of men who helped mold modern journalism by building what became the Scripps-Howard newspaper chain. She wanted nothing to do with the family business, and when she was barely out of her teens, she eloped with an older man. Their marriage was unhappy and short-lived, ending in a much-publicized divorce after she fell in love with William Loeb, already an ambitious, unconventional newspaper publisher. She quickly became his business partner, albeit one who preferred to work behind the scenes. Throughout their marriage, she served in a variety of informal roles, consulting on both newspaper operations and editorial stances. "Bill and I were a team operation," she said a few years after his death. "We read the mail. We played lousy tennis. We talked politics. We hiked. We made plans, and we tried to make them work."[5]

Nackey eschewed the spotlight; those who knew her often describe her as an introvert. But she would break her silence and contribute to the national political conversation whenever she thought her voice would benefit the conservative movement. An ardent anti-communist, Nackey tussled publicly in the early 1950s with Scripps-Howard executives—including her older brother—over how the chain was covering Senator Joseph McCarthy, accusing the papers of "rotten, biased journalism."[6] A few years later, amid the crisis over attempts to integrate Central High School in Little Rock, Arkansas, she drew an editorial cartoon objecting to the use of federal troops to escort African American students through crowds of angry, white protesters. The image—titled "Brotherhood by Bayonet!"—quickly became popular among segregationist groups, appearing on posters and bumper stickers and in a magazine published by the White Citizens' Council.[7]

Together, the Loebs used New Hampshire's first-in-the-nation presidential primary to vault themselves into the national political arena, becoming an important part of the conservative media ecosystem that emerged during the middle of the twentieth century.[8] They dined at Nixon's White House, entertained ambitious politicians, and sat for dozens of interviews with reporters curious about the people behind what Pat Buchanan once described as "the paper liberals fear to read." Nackey spent decades helping to turn the *Union Leader* and its Sunday edition, the *New Hampshire Sunday News*, into a political powerhouse, while also raising two daughters and managing the family's Nevada ranch and Massachusetts mansion. As William Loeb's health declined, her role grew. By the end of his life, she was writing many of the letters he signed.[9] When she took over as publisher in the fall of 1981, Nackey was well known and, in many conservative circles, well respected.

Still, her first few years as publisher were full of challenges. There was widespread skepticism about her ability to do the job, and rumors spread that the *Union Leader* was rudderless and powerless without its fiery former owner. While she was proving herself as both a manager and a political influencer, she was also contending with a host of complicated operational challenges caused by outdated equipment, growing circulation, and rapid changes to both communication technology and New Hampshire's media landscape—a reality that led her to move the newspaper out of its downtown building and into a new, modern plant that she helped design.

She said often that she was grateful to have inherited a competent team of managers to help her through this time, but she also drew on the strength and self-confidence she'd discovered while recovering from a near-fatal car accident. In 1977 she was gravely injured in a Jeep rollover that left her paralyzed from the chest down. She spent many grueling months in rehab and needed a wheelchair for the rest of her life. Her injuries were devastating and forced her to make hard decisions about where to devote her limited energy, but she also credited the experience with preparing her to run the *Union Leader*. "In the last few years of Bill's life," she once said, "when things were getting more difficult, and I had to face the future, I don't know whether I would have been able to handle that if I hadn't been toughened by making my place in this wheelchair."[10]

Nackey is perhaps best known for her editorials; she wrote more than 1,600 during her tenure. But her most interesting and enduring activism took place behind the scenes as she cultivated audiences, connected like-minded activists, and recruited presidential candidates— sometimes successfully, sometimes not. She used her editorials and regular appearances on national television to build her power by crafting a quirky, smart, hard-right persona that attracted a loyal and widespread following. Most of her career predated digital publishing, so she devoted time and resources to amplifying the paper's ideological voice via print, at one point publishing a popular (and free) national opinion newsletter and sometimes arranging to fly copies of the *Union Leader* to Capitol Hill. This made Nackey and her newspaper important touchstones for conservative activists and a common target for those who opposed her views. Her editorials were quoted in campaign ads, read into the *Congressional Record*, and reprinted in major newspapers around the world. Her audience was widespread, loyal, and crucial to the rise of many right-wing candidates, including Pat Buchanan.

Although largely beyond the scope of this book, Nackey's personal life was fascinating too. She was a crack shot, an accomplished horsewoman, and an avid outdoor adventurer who used a special off-road wheelchair to get to her favorite fly-fishing spots in the years after her accident. Her artistic talents were vast and varied, and she could fix just about anything—always an impressive skill but, as her daughter pointed out, even more so in the years before DIY YouTube videos. Animals, especially bulldogs, were an important part of her life, and she once nursed a duck with a broken wing back to health, first in the bathtub and later in the swimming pool.[11] She adored her three grandchildren and often interrupted interviews, business meetings, and political strategy sessions to brag about their latest exploits.

In the final years of her life, Nackey grew concerned about who would run the *Union Leader* after she was gone. She also worried that average citizens, especially teenagers, were uninformed about the First Amendment and the role of the press in democracy. The solution to both problems came in the form of the Nackey S. Loeb School of Communications, a nonprofit that was created in 1999.[12] The school, which is the primary owner of the Union Leader Corporation, operates out of a Manchester office suite that used to house a truck-driving academy. It offers regular classes and workshops, most of them free and all of them designed to educate everyday people about open records laws, free speech, journalism, photography, public relations, and more. Each year it gives a First Amendment award in Nackey's name.

It was there, more than a decade ago, that I first learned about Nackey's influence when I was invited to teach a writing workshop at the school. That experience started the slow career pivot that led me to become a journalism professor. It's also the reason why you're holding this book. I was—and still am—a political junkie, a news nerd, and a proud New Hampshire native, but I knew little about Nackey beyond her unusual first name and the fact that she'd been married to William Loeb. Curious, I looked around for her biography, and when I discovered that one did not exist, I began investigating her family, her work at the newspaper, and her impact on conservative politics.

At first I assumed that the historical record included very little about Nackey, which would explain why her life had not been more thoroughly documented. That was not the case, and researching this book turned into a scavenger hunt through time. I found relevant materials in nearly a dozen archives, most notably C-SPAN's online video library, the E. W. Scripps Collection at Ohio University, and some of Nackey's personal papers, which are stored in stacks of bankers boxes at the school. Nackey's papers are what librarians call "unprocessed," which means they lack a standard organizational structure, but I've done my best in the endnotes to be specific and transparent about which documents I've cited. I also spoke to dozens of people—some on the record, some off—about various aspects of Nackey's life, career, and influence. On-the-record interviews are cited contextually or in the endnotes. Off-the-record interviews were used to track down documents or verify facts. I've avoided anonymous sources. It's also important to note that this book is an independent endeavor produced without editorial input from the Loeb School or the Union Leader Corporation. That said, I am grateful for the time and access granted to me by the school and by the newspaper's employees, both current and former.

Also crucial in my research were the many public statements Nackey made about her paralysis. Wherever possible, I've used direct quotes to describe Nackey's experience as a person with a disability. In other places, I've relied on information provided by Nackey's eldest daughter, Nackey Scagliotti. Terminology about disabilities has evolved since the 1980s, and I've used modern standards in my own writing. Words in direct quotes reflect contemporary norms. Readers will also notice that I refer to Nackey by her first name. In doing so, I mean no disrespect. She had three last names during her life—Scripps, Loeb, and Gallowhur (the surname of her first husband). By using her first name, I endeavor to bring consistency to the narrative and to distinguish her from other people in her family.

This is not a book about William Loeb, but his colorful and controversial career was a significant factor in Nackey's adult life, and his purchase of the *Union Leader* is what launched them both onto the national stage. His larger-than-life persona inspired many magazine and newspaper profiles and at least two books about his career and political influence. In some cases he disputed the facts presented and took the authors to court. Wherever possible, I've used multiple sources to verify information about his life. I also rely heavily on a 2001 documentary produced by New Hampshire Public Television in consultation with respected historian (and former Granite Stater) Michael J. Birkner and a group of Loeb's friends, foes, and family members.

During the time I've spent writing this book, many people have asked me what I think of Nackey. Here's my answer: She was a smart businesswoman with a fascinating backstory who displayed amazing tenacity throughout her life, especially after her Jeep accident. She was a careful student of the issues of her day and believed she was using her powerful position to advance her idea of a free society. She valued civic engagement and strong, independent local newspapers. That said, I find many aspects of her ideology troubling, even when viewed through the lens of the time in which she lived. Particularly problematic to me are the stances she took that enabled segregationist and homophobic practices. This book is not an endorsement of her philosophy but rather an exploration of the impact of a powerful and unique media personality. Like many of her critics, I also wish she had been more open to feminism. Nackey was a rare female leader in the male-dominated world of newspapering, but she was not a feminist. She editorialized against the Equal Rights Amendment and dismissed members of the movement as "women's libbers."

Women's roles in journalism are generally described in progressive terms: plucky stunt girls like Nellie Bly, activists who used their printing presses to rally support for suffrage, brave war correspondents who negotiated access to the front lines, journalists at major news organizations who won equal-pay lawsuits. Nackey, meanwhile, pushed boundaries by participating in the largely male arenas of publishing and politics, but she advocated for the status quo or, in some cases, a return to more reactionary social norms related to gender and race. Exploring that tension is part of a full inquiry into the many ways women have contributed to civic life and shaped the evolution of modern politics. As recent work by historians, political scientists, and journalists has revealed, there are many ways in which women, most of them white, Christian, and financially secure, have influenced and, in some cases, even defined conservative thought over the last century.

Despite Nackey's dismissal of the need for more policies that support gender equity, there is nevertheless a feminist case to be made for documenting her career. Her near eradication from the collective understanding of New Hampshire's presidential primary and its role in national politics is an example of what feminist scholars call symbolic annihilation, a phenomenon in which mass media tends to build narratives that omit, condemn, or trivialize women.[13] In a 2001 academic essay, the prominent journalism historian Maurine Beasley argued that many women working in journalism have been overlooked in part because they're seen as subordinate to male relatives. "Such women are rarely given more than a superficial mention, if that, in American journalism history because they are not seen as legitimate practitioners," Beasley wrote. "Do they deserve more?"[14]

In the case of Nackey Scripps Loeb, the answer is yes.

Legacy   1

There's a joke among politicos that the next New Hampshire primary starts about halfway through a new president-elect's victory speech. An exaggeration, for sure; but after Ronald Reagan won his second term in 1984, the Republican Party's right wing wanted to get a jump on the 1988 election. Conservative activists saw Reagan's ascendance as a huge and hard-fought victory, one their movement had been working toward for decades. The end of his presidency marked a crossroads for the GOP. Would the party continue to tack rightward? Or would it embrace a more moderate candidate with a centrist agenda? The tension between these competing visions of Republicanism wasn't new. It manifested over and over during the second half of the twentieth century, and loud echoes of this fight reverberate today. One important salvo took place in early December 1985 at a tony fundraiser in downtown Washington DC, where political power brokers assembled to watch a newspaper publisher named Nackey Scripps Loeb pay tribute to her late husband.

She had been invited to speak by Max Hugel, a square-faced, well-connected New Hampshire businessman who had worked for Reagan's campaign. Hugel had just launched a new political action committee, Project '88: Americans for the Reagan Agenda, and was funneling money to right-leaning candidates mounting midterm campaigns in key states. He hoped the banquet would bring in more cash, and he wanted to make a show of conservative strength. To attract both guests and media attention, he branded the evening as a celebration of William Loeb, Nackey's husband of twenty-nine years, who, even in death, remained a source of fascination for the political class.

Among right-wing activists, the Loebs were folk heroes. Their foes, meanwhile, saw them as eccentric agitators clinging to outdated and sometimes bigoted ideals. Much of their life together had centered on turning their *Union Leader* into a powerhouse, using the growing influence of New Hampshire's first-in-the-nation presidential primary to vault themselves into the national political arena. William Loeb was hyperbolic, hyper-conservative, and prone to what one political scientist called "editorial pyrotechnics."[1] His personal life was complicated— Nackey was his third wife—and his father, also William Loeb, had been famous, serving as Teddy Roosevelt's personal secretary. The younger William shot guns and rode horses, and when it came to his front-page editorials, he pulled no punches, lobbing insults like "Dopey Dwight" (President Eisenhower); "a pious, pompous fraud" (Martin Luther King Jr.); and "Moscow Maggie" (Senator Margaret Chase Smith).

Nackey's backstory was just as fascinating. She was an heiress to the Scripps newspaper fortune, a prolific artist, and an accomplished horsewoman who kept a pistol in her purse and, as one journalist noted, was the best shot in the family.[2] During William Loeb's life, Nackey served as his mostly silent business partner, making the occasional public splash with a political cartoon or editorial of her own. When he died in 1981, she assumed control of the Union Leader Corporation's daily operations and political maneuvering.

Nackey wasn't the only high-profile speaker at Hugel's dinner. Vice President George H. W. Bush had agreed to give the keynote address— something that surprised many people, especially Nackey. She had no problem with Bush as a person. ("Delightful," she once called him. "Very much of a gentleman.")[3] But the Loebs and the Bushes had long aligned themselves with different factions of the GOP. The vice president's father, Senator Prescott Bush, opposed Joseph McCarthy's anti-communist crusade, supported school desegregation, and was associated with Planned Parenthood in the 1940s. As the younger Bush's political profile grew, he too sometimes gravitated toward the political center, such as when he signaled support for the Equal Rights Amendment (ERA) in the early 1970s. (After becoming Reagan's running mate, Bush backed off on the ERA and shifted his public rhetoric rightward, but most conservatives saw this as a testament to his loyalty, not a change in his personal politics.)

The Loebs embraced and helped define a more extreme conservative ideology, using the *Union Leader* to inject its tenets into the national political conversation. Over the years, the couple championed not just McCarthy but also southern segregationists, hard-right presidential hopefuls like Barry Goldwater, and the anti-feminist efforts of Phyllis Schlafly. They railed against elite—and, in their minds, overly liberal—colleges, accused major news organizations of left-leaning bias, and believed the United States would be better off if everyone were a little more religious. The Loebs were also early and ardent supporters of Reagan, repeatedly torpedoing other Republican candidates on the front page of their *Union Leader* and, in Nackey's case, writing glowing columns about his wife, Nancy.[4] One of William Loeb's favorite targets during the 1980 New Hampshire primary was Bush. In editorial after editorial, Loeb called him terrible things: "incompetent," "unfit," and a "spoiled little rich kid." He also deemed him soft on communism and suggested voters treat the Bush campaign "as if it were the black plague itself."[5]

When word got out that Loeb's widow would share a head table with one of the *Union Leader*'s favorite ideological nemeses, reporters from around the country clamored to cover the story. It was delicious political theater that illustrated divisions within the GOP both nationally and in the home of the first primary. Rumors circulated that Hugel's real goal was to discourage Bush from mounting a presidential bid, although he insisted Project '88's only aim was to give conservatives an opportunity to test the waters and consider entering the race. The PAC wasn't the only thing that made Hugel a polarizing figure. He'd known the Loebs for years, sharing their affinity for both conservatism and horses. His work on the Reagan campaign earned him an appointment to the CIA, but he resigned soon after accusations surfaced that he had improperly handled stock transactions. Nackey rushed to Hugel's defense, writing in an editorial that he was a "patriot and a believer in the American dream" whose reputation had been tarnished by liberal media bias.[6] The charges against Hugel were never proven, and he later won a libel suit against his accusers, but he never returned to his government post. Instead, he joined an effort to rehabilitate a struggling horse track on the Granite State's southern border—a project Nackey supported in her editorials multiple times.

She'd supported him again when, shortly before launching his PAC, Hugel made an unsuccessful bid for chair of the New Hampshire Republican Party. His campaign drew criticism from members of the party worried that he would make it hard for moderate candidates to run successfully in the Granite State. By endorsing his candidacy, Nackey had, for neither the first time nor the last, put herself at odds with many of the state's establishment Republicans.[7] In the weeks before the dinner, some complained publicly that Hugel's new PAC was siphoning money that could be put to better use by the state party.[8] All of this—plus the usual pre-primary political posturing—set the scene for an awkward evening. As *Conservative Digest* founder Richard Vigerie put it a few weeks before the dinner, "Anybody who is anybody in conservative politics has agreed to attend. I can't think of an event in recent years that has so much irony in it. . . . There will be a lot of people there who don't think too highly of each other, smiling at each other and having their picture taken together."[9]

Fancy dinners weren't really Nackey's style, and although she loved to travel, it had become logistically challenging after a 1977 car accident left her paralyzed from the chest down. As she often said, she could do a lot from her wheelchair, but she still had to conserve her energy. The dinner, she decided, was worth the effort, so she accepted Hugel's invitation. A tribute to William Loeb was flattering, and such a high-profile event would be good for her newspaper's brand and, by extension, its political clout. The banquet, she wrote to a friend, "proved that people are very anxious about the New Hampshire primary and also want to curry favor with the *Union Leader*. I will try to keep them very concerned about what we might or might not say about them."[10]

Bush's motivations for attending were equally strategic. Plenty of

Republicans thought it was foolish for him to go, but members of his inner circle convinced him that appearing at the dinner would be helpful as he ramped up his presidential campaign. He needed to court conservatives, many of whom doubted his right-wing bona fides, and this would be a good place to start. A strong showing might also dissuade other potential candidates from launching campaigns of their own.[11]

Nackey was just as conservative as her late husband, but her thoughts on the 1988 race—and Bush—were an open question. In the weeks before the dinner, she received multiple phone calls from curious reporters. She kept publicly mum on the vice president's chances with the *Union Leader* but reached out to Bush privately. "As you know, Bill and I haven't always seen eye to eye with you politically, but he would have admired your loyalty to the President, as do I, and he would be most honored by your presence at the dinner," she wrote in a letter. "Naturally there are those who will try to create an issue out of all of this if they can. I'm told some are already busy at it, looking up some of Bill's tougher editorial comments when we were backing your 'boss' against you. Well, so what? Bill would have chuckled. I feel the same, and I suspect you do, too. I just wanted you to know that this in no way lessens my pleasure that you will be playing a part in the upcoming occasion."[12]

It's unclear if Bush replied, but he had plenty of opportunity to chat with Nackey at the dinner. The two were seated side by side at a head table reserved for members of Reagan's administration and top Republicans from states with early primaries. Except for Barbara Bush and Nackey, all of the honored guests were men. A big banner with the Project '88 logo hung above the stage, and the dining area was packed with people who wanted to be president or work for a future president someday. Tickets sold for $250 apiece. A half dozen potential presidential candidates, including Jeane Kirkpatrick, Bob Dole, and Jack Kemp, signed on as sponsors. The press corps was robust, and C-SPAN broadcast the entire event, zooming in often on Nackey and the vice president. Nackey was thrilled with the size of the audience and amused by what she later described as the "political one-upmanship games" going on in the ballroom. Her late husband, she thought, would have found the scene fascinating.[13] The caliber of the potential candidates, however, was disappointing. "Ronald Reagan," she lamented in a letter to a friend, "is a hard act to follow."[14]

Shortly after the coffee was served, Bush stepped up to the lectern. His keynote was a pep talk for the upcoming midterms, laced with self-effacing humor about his less-than-warm relationship with William Loeb. "He wasn't always my biggest fan," Bush said. "I could tell when we were in trouble in New Hampshire in 1980. I'd send the dog out in the morning to fetch the *Union Leader*, and he'd try to hide it." He listed some of the names he'd been called during his various campaigns and attempted to bolster his conservative credentials by stressing that he was the target not just of the *Union Leader* but of liberal publications too. "Rough and tumble is part of American political life," he said. "When the campaign is over, you forget what was said in the heat of battle, you shake hands, and, win or lose, you get on with the cause of making the country better for our children and their children."

Nackey spoke from behind a bank of microphones arranged for her on the head table. She adjusted her glasses, shuffled her notes, and waved casually at the room. The turnout, she said, would have pleased her late husband, but he'd have been furious that no one in the newspaper's contingent thought to bring a stack of blank subscription cards to pass around. (The *Union Leader*'s audience stretched far beyond the Granite State, and many far-flung readers received their papers by mail.) "He would say, 'Readership like that, what a waste!'" She vowed that, come 1988, she would support whatever candidate best embodied Reagan-style conservatism. "Whether that person is here tonight remains to be seen." She cracked a few jokes, shared a few memories of her long marriage, and declared, "Bill wouldn't say it, but I'm going say it. I believe that perhaps the state of New Hampshire and the United States of America are a little better for the *Union Leader* being here."[15]

Nackey's speech earned a standing ovation. As the men around her clapped, she grinned and, from her wheelchair, used both arms to thrust a copy of the *Union Leader* high into the air above her head.[16] To casual observers, it was a spunky tribute to her late husband. For the conservatives assembled in the room, it was as if she were holding aloft a battle flag. For George Bush, it was a harbinger of the trouble Nackey and her powerful newspaper would cause him in the years to come.

For Nackey, the Project '88 dinner also marked a personal victory, one that signaled her efforts to remain a force in the national political landscape were working. When she took over as publisher, she had resources, experience, and a deep commitment to both local news and the conservative cause. Still, there was no shortage of people who thought she wasn't up to the task. As the granddaughter, daughter, and wife of newspapermen, she knew the business well and had been a respected figure among right-wing activists for decades. But Nackey Scripps Loeb—a petite woman with short silver hair who needed a wheelchair to get around—didn't *look* like most people's idea of a publisher, much less one who could spark fear among politicians who strayed too far from conservative ideals.

Even today, politics and journalism are overwhelmingly male arenas, but in the early 1980s, they were more overtly hostile to women.[17] At the same time, people with disabilities remained largely absent from public life, and when they did appear, they were often marginalized or infantilized. In Nackey's case, these dynamics coalesced into a sexist, ableist narrative that persisted in the years after the death of her husband. The journalists who documented her rise to the position of publisher did so with skepticism, predicting that even if she could manage her new responsibilities, the *Union Leader* would soon lose its clout. A *New York Times* headline proclaimed, "Loeb's Paper Serves New Hampshire Less Venom."[18] The *Boston Globe* was more blunt: "Because Nackey Loeb has been paralyzed from the waist down since 1977, the result of a Nevada Jeep accident, few observers feel she will be able to exercise the same level of control over the paper."[19]

Nackey confronted not just stereotypes about gender and disability but also lasting reverberations of her late husband's legacy. Democrats despised him. Republicans feared him. National political reporters saw him as an irresistible story, one they loved to revisit every four years. In profiles and prime-time TV broadcasts, journalists would examine his words and guess what impact they might have on the outcome of that year's presidential race. When he died on September 13, 1981, they pondered the future of the Union Leader Corporation both as a business enterprise and as a political actor. "New England," wrote the *New York Times*, "is awash in the legend of his vitriolic power and in speculation about what changes his absence might bring."[20]

While it's certainly fair to ponder how new leadership might change a media company like the *Union Leader*, the frequent comparisons between Nackey and William Loeb missed an important dynamic. Nackey Scripps Loeb wasn't just her husband's successor. She was also a crucial part of their newspaper's rise to prominence, working alongside William Loeb in a variety of informal, behind-the-scenes roles. As the granddaughter of newspaper baron E. W. Scripps, Nackey understood the publishing business, and she drew on that expertise—and the Scripps family resources—throughout her career. She evaluated would-be presidents, helped shape the paper's editorial stance, and managed the mail—no small task given the hundreds of letters her husband received in a typical week. Nackey did all of this while raising two daughters and running the family's homes.

Still, when William Loeb died, no one would have questioned Nackey if she'd given up her leadership role, serving as a figurehead or even selling the paper to one of the big media chains that would have loved a foothold in such a politically important state. Instead, she decided to reshape her life and embrace a big and very public job. She wanted to honor her husband's legacy and continue providing local news to New Hampshire residents, but she also believed it was her duty to keep the *Union Leader* strong, independent, and conservative. That meant Nackey had to embrace multiple roles: local newspaper publisher, right-wing commentator, behind-the-scenes political adviser, and as the national news landscape underwent massive change in the 1980s and 1990s, media innovator. She considered the newspaper a member of her family, so becoming its top executive felt like a natural process rather than a burden. "Bill and I shared a great deal of the responsibilities to it," she said. "We thought very much alike."[21]

On a personal level, Nackey probably didn't care what anyone thought about her ability to run the *Union Leader*. She knew that day-to-day management was going well: Her executive team was smart and collegial, circulation and advertising were on the rise, and the company was finally addressing long-festering problems with its production equipment. But Nackey's new job involved a lot more than tending to practicalities. The *Union Leader* was also a political organ. As its publisher, Nackey was now the public face and chief editorial voice of the operation, and her success as a political power broker depended on how she was perceived. Within days of her husband's death, while his funeral plans were still under way, she began building her public persona by continuing his tradition of front-page editorials. In her first column as publisher, she wrote that William Loeb "spoke out frankly and straightforwardly against any weakening of the basic values on which all our lives should be based." The paper, she said, would continue to do the same under her leadership. "We are not merely a product but a team of very able people with a single purpose—to produce the best newspaper possible to best serve the people of New Hampshire and the citizens of this country."[22]

Nackey had never been one to seek publicity; those who knew her well describe her as an introvert. But she maintained a robust speaking schedule during her first year as publisher, spending many hours reassuring local readers that the newspaper was in good hands. At a meeting of the North Shore Press Club in Salem, Massachusetts, she reported that circulation was rising.[23] In New Hampshire, she told the Manchester Girls Club that her company was thriving and dismissed what she called "prophets telling the world that the paper will never be the same and that it will sink into oblivion."[24] At the annual luncheon of the New Hampshire Federation of Business and Professional Women, she tossed aside prepared remarks to chat with the audience. One member complained that the federation's press releases appeared on the *Union Leader*'s women's pages instead of in the business section with news from other professional groups. Nackey agreed that seemed unfair. "I will talk to the editors," she said, "and tell them they're a bunch of chauvinists."[25]

Slowly, Nackey's profile began to rise. Her public appearances helped, but it was her front-page editorials that really attracted attention. Although she was less prone to name calling than her husband, she made it clear that she had no intention of sitting on the political sidelines. She wrote forcefully and frequently about the evils of communism, the benefits of low taxes, and the problem with congressional junkets.[26] Her photo began to appear too: a black-and-white portrait with an expression that, while serious, hinted at her unpretentious demeanor and fondness for corny jokes. Each editorial concluded with her thin, looping signature, a personal touch that made many readers feel as if she were speaking directly to them.

One regular reader of Nackey's editorials was Ronald Reagan. She and the president had been friends for years. The *Union Leader* endorsed him in his unsuccessful presidential bid in 1976 and again when he won in 1980. As his first term progressed, she became a sort of informal adviser to him. In regular letters and occasional phone calls, she offered her thoughts on staff appointments, policy matters, and campaign messaging. Her editorials were a focal point of their conversations; she'd often enclose copies with her letters. Sometimes, if the issue was especially urgent, she'd use overnight mail to get her ideas on his desk quickly.[27] Their letters were friendly, a little cheeky, and generally casual. Nackey almost never called him Mr. President, choosing instead to open with "Dear Ron." Reagan respected her opinion and her position, once calling her "one of the leading members of the Fourth Estate."[28]

Despite her friendship with Reagan, Nackey didn't hide her frustrations with his administration. In early 1982 she wrote an editorial advising him to ignore members of his staff who were, in her eyes, moderating his policies. "The people of this country elected Ronald Reagan because of his views and beliefs, not in spite of them," she wrote.

"What they don't want is for yet another President to be swallowed up in the Washington hooey." She sent him a copy, and a few days later, Reagan responded: "How good it is to hear from you even if you did give me a polite spanking," the president wrote. "From you, I'll take it and like it."[29] Later that year, after the GOP performed poorly in the midterms, Nackey, like many other conservatives, worried that the new political opposition would force Reagan to moderate his policies. She sent him a few notes and, when she was unsatisfied with his response, made her criticism public.

In an open letter published on January 19, 1983, Nackey warned Reagan that any departure from the conservative agenda he laid out during his campaign could cost him her support. "The *Union Leader*, under the leadership of my late husband, believed in a strong, safe America and within it the financial freedom of every American to build his or her own future, and that is what the Reagan platform was all about," she wrote. "We still believe in that platform; but I am very fearful that perhaps Ronald Reagan may have abandoned it. . . . I will continue to support, with the *Union Leader*, the platform you promised. But I will not support ANYONE who abandons it."[30]

She sent a copy of the editorial to the White House, and Reagan's staff got worried. Although the president remained fairly popular in New Hampshire and beyond, Nackey's editorial wasn't just ideological saber rattling. The *Union Leader* had a habit of supporting challengers to incumbents who didn't pass conservative muster—something many members of Reagan's inner circle likely recalled from 1976, when the Loebs backed Reagan's attempt to snatch the nomination away from President Gerald Ford. (Four years earlier, in 1972, the paper backed Ohio congressman John Ashbrook's unsuccessful attempt to topple Richard Nixon.)[31] The *Union Leader* didn't always pick winners in its endorsements, but its wrath could be costly to candidates. Members of Reagan's team knew their road to re-election would be a lot easier with Nackey and her newspaper on their side.[32]

Reagan was scheduled to visit Boston a few weeks after the "Dear Ron" letter, and his staff decided to try to patch things up with Nackey by arranging a face-to-face. It was his first visit to the city since taking office, and he would be on the ground for less than half a day. The schedule was already packed with events intended to promote high-tech job training programs for people living in the socioeconomically depressed Roxbury neighborhood, but the president's handlers still found time for Nackey.

The two met at a massive production facility belonging to Digital Equipment Corporation. Reagan arrived aboard the Marine One heli-copter and was trailed by the usual presidential entourage. Nackey made the fifty-mile trip from Manchester, New Hampshire, in a wheel-chair van she'd nicknamed the Foxy Lady. She was accompanied by her new editor in chief, Joe McQuaid, a young, lanky, third-generation newspaperman who was already rather fond of his unconventional boss. Thick crowds surrounded the building. Protesters waved signs reading "Bread Not Bombs" and "Boston Needs Jobs, Housing, Food." There were supporters of the president, too, many of whom applauded his arrival.[33] Security was tight, but when the Secret Service saw Nack-ey's wheelchair, they waved her around the metal detectors and ushered her inside.

When Reagan arrived, Nackey insisted on speaking to him alone and shooed everyone else out of the room. James Baker, Reagan's chief of staff, lingered in an open doorway, and Nackey grew frustrated. She viewed his hovering as more evidence of what she considered the White House staff's over-management of the president. "I was tempted to call out 'Come in, Mr. Baker. You can hear a lot better in here,'" Nackey later wrote in a letter, "but good manners took over, and I did not say anything." (Nackey wasn't alone in her frustration. The refrain "let Reagan be Reagan" became a rallying cry for conservatives during his administration.)[34] The meeting was quick, and the van was soon headed back north. Inside, Nackey reached into her purse, pulled out the pistol she usually carried, and casually passed it up to the driver. "Here," McQuaid remembers her saying. "You can put this away now."[35]

The meeting wasn't on the president's official schedule, but Nackey made sure it was soon a matter of public knowledge. The next morning, the *Union Leader* splashed a photo of Nackey and Reagan across the front page under the headline "The President and the Publisher." In it, she's talking and using her hands to emphasize a point as he leans in to listen. There is no known transcript of their conversation, but the substance mattered less than what the image telegraphed: Nackey Scripps Loeb had a lot to say, and politicians hoping to maintain their credibility among conservatives were wise to pay attention.

Nackey was pleased with the trip's outcome, writing in a letter that the attention she received from the White House "certainly indicates the newspaper is still considered important as far as the political world is concerned."[36] Coverage of Nackey began to change almost immediately. The photo was syndicated through a national wire service and was reprinted in, among other places, the *Boston Globe*, which called the meeting the "Reagan-Loeb summit" and challenged the narrative that the *Union Leader* was no longer a force in conservative politics. In fact, some readers wondered if Nackey's milder tone might make her *more* powerful than her late husband. One politician who made this argument was Philip Crane, an Illinois congressman who had been the target of repeated attacks by William Loeb during an unsuccessful presidential bid in 1980. Being on the receiving end of critical editorials was terrible, Crane said, but William Loeb's vitriolic reputation made him fairly easy to discredit. The same wasn't true under the new publisher. "If Nackey is more subtle," he said, "the paper may lose something in the way of its traditional spice, but it might be more credible."[37]

Nackey's editorial voice wasn't the only asset that helped her build her audience and connect with conservatives across the country who were clamoring for a bigger media ecosystem. The first few years of her tenure as publisher coincided with profound changes in the national news landscape. Big television stations and cable news became more significant parts of Americans' media diet, and as the 1984 election cycle opened, they were all vying for a piece of the action. This gave Nackey an unprecedented opportunity to amplify her voice.

One key player in this arena was C-SPAN. During Reagan's reelection campaign, Nackey became a frequent and popular guest. The network launched in 1979, but it didn't start regular remote coverage until the 1984 election cycle, broadcasting 176 hours of live and taped programming related to the Iowa caucuses and New Hampshire primary.[38] Susan Swain was among the many C-SPAN journalists who visited the Granite State that year, and she spent several days observing operations at the *Union Leader* for a documentary. In a column published in C-SPAN's newsletter, she recalled the intense attention the paper received from other news organizations. "We are constantly meeting print and broadcast journalists filing reports from the newspaper's offices," she wrote. "One day, as our camera crew was videotaping outside the *Union Leader* building, a reporter looked over and said 'This is the media, watching the media, watching the media.'"[39]

The documentary, "A Day in the Life of the *Union Leader*," aired on February 21, 1984. It was classic C-SPAN: unfiltered, full of jump cuts, and utterly fascinating despite its slow pace. Viewers saw hours of footage from inside the *Union Leader* headquarters, including forty-five minutes of Nackey leading a weekly department head meeting. Men wearing suits and carrying stacks of papers crowded around her enormous desk, scribbling notes and answering her questions. She was the only woman in the camera frame.[40] Nackey also sat for a long on-air interview with C-SPAN founder Brian Lamb. He was thrilled to meet her and remembers how kind she was to everyone on the set. But he was still a little intimidated when they met. "It's not a negative," he said. "That's just how strong she was. . . . She enjoyed being tough with strong opinions. Didn't care what anybody thought. Wasn't looking to be a star. Just did her thing."[41]

Lamb interviewed Nackey live for about an hour, pausing to take phone calls from viewers. Most of the conversation focused on the 1984 primary and the history of the *Union Leader*, which, Lamb told the audience, had "probably gotten more publicity than any paper in the country."[42] C-SPAN viewers were enamored of Nackey, and dozens called in during the broadcast. Even the ones who didn't agree with her politics found her interesting. "Mrs. Loeb is just charming," said a man who called in from Houston. "I was never much a fan of her husband, but obviously, he had good taste."[43] The fascination with Nackey was widespread and lasting. In the days after the primary, the *Union Leader*'s circulation department received hundreds of out-of-state requests for mail subscriptions, with especially intense interest from the South and the Midwest.

Far-flung subscribers were nothing new for the paper—it was serving an estimated three thousand out-of-state readers at the time—but the attention the paper received during the 1984 primary expanded the audience.[44] Many new subscribers sent notes with their checks, complimenting Nackey and complaining about what they saw as liberal bias in their own local newspapers. "We were so impressed by all the people we met on C-SPAN, especially Mrs. Nackey Loeb," wrote a couple in Florida. "We know we want to receive the paper in our home." A new fan in Michigan applauded Nackey and hoped she would "live a good long life" as publisher. From Maryland someone professed, "Your paper, Mrs. Loeb and staff, renewed my faith in America."[45]

While Nackey's speeches and meetings with political elites fortified her reputation as a political power broker, it was her ability to forge deep and personal connections with rank-and-file conservatives that defined her career. The audience she built was eclectic, sprawling, and frustrated with the status quo. They were her champions, her analog social network, and when she decided to push the GOP even further to the right, the source of her power.

Family Business   2

Nackey Loeb never wanted to run a newspaper. In fact, she often joked that she spent her childhood plotting an escape from the publishing empire built by her grandfather, E. W. Scripps. He died just after Nackey's second birthday, so she knew him mostly by reputation, but his business interests and personal eccentricities shaped the contours of her unusual childhood.[1] When she was born on February 24, 1924, the Scripps newspaper chain sprawled from coast to coast, with properties in roughly two dozen communities.[2] Management had passed to her father, Robert Paine Scripps, and his job required frequent travel. Her mother, Margaret, often followed with a growing brood of children and their nannies in tow. Before Nackey was six months old, she'd made her first cross-country journey. As she grew older, she delighted in train trips, waking up in her bunk to the sound of clacking wheels and watching out the window as towns and farms whizzed by.[3] Wherever the family went, newspaper executives would soon appear for business meetings, social events, or both. "All they did was talk about papers," she said. "It bored me to death."[4]

Born in 1854 in Rushville, Illinois, Edward Willis Scripps was a key figure in the golden age of newspaper barons. Along with men like Joseph Pulitzer and William Randolph Hearst, he spent the late nineteenth and early twentieth centuries revolutionizing the "industry's organization, operations and norms."[5] Pulitzer innovated with content, creating newspapers packed with stories designed for mass audience appeal, mixing lively page design with hard-hitting investigative journalism. Hearst built upon this work, adding tabloid spice through coverage of entertainment, salacious crime, and splashy stunts designed to make headlines. Scripps created the infrastructure of news, pioneering chain ownership and launching wire services. He became "the prototype of the modern publisher, concentrating on long-range planning, performance goals, budgets, circulation methods, revenue sources and a broad range of other business concerns."[6]

His company—which had several names during his tenure but is best known as Scripps-Howard—was the first newspaper chain in the United States and included dozens of publications targeted at working-class readers in small and medium-sized cities. He also established three wire services: United Press International; a features syndicate called the Newspaper Enterprise Association; and the Science Service, which provided explanatory science news to members. Scripps viewed his papers as tools for civic engagement among rank-and-file Americans, designed to counter a big-city press he felt was too elite.[7] When it came to politics, he and his newspapers avoided strong partisan ties, although a series of essays he wrote later in life illustrated his left-leaning world view.[8]

The publishing business was lucrative for E.W., and he devoted some of his vast fortune to building an eclectic family compound outside of San Diego. Called Miramar, it stretched across ten thousand acres and included dozens of buildings interspersed with generators, reservoirs, and water cisterns. The climate was arid, and the land was covered with eucalyptus trees, lemon groves, and cacti. The newspaper chain was officially based in Cincinnati, but E.W. preferred to work from home, so he built guest quarters for visiting editors, directors, and other corporate leaders. The ranch wasn't opulent, but signs abounded of the Scripps family fortune: fleets of cars and motorcycles; horses for both work and show; a massive bunk house for servants, tutors, and groundskeepers; an aviary; a gym; and a big patio for open-air dances. The neighbors weren't quite sure what to think of it and considered the kids who lived there rather wild, part of "a three-ring circus featuring riding, swimming, hiking, cycling, cow-pie tossing, motorcycle races, and catching rattlesnakes."[9]

In 1885 E.W. married Natalie Holtsinger, the daughter of a Presbyterian minister from rural Ohio. She called herself Nackie—a name that has been given to generations of Scripps women, albeit with a slightly altered spelling. They had six children: James George, John Paul, Dorothy "Dolla" Blair, Edward Willis, Robert Paine, and Nackey Elizabeth.[10] E.W. was mercurial both as a parent and as a manager. He frequently pitted his children against each other, causing deep and occasionally litigious rifts within the family business. It was during one such feud that control of the newspaper chain shifted to Nackey's father, Bob. For many years, the company had been led by E.W.'s eldest son, James, but when James finally lost patience with his moody, hard-to-please father, he left the business, taking seven West Coast papers with him. E.W. was furious and, in 1922, installed Bob as the chain's editorial director. The change left Nackey's father, who was just twenty-seven years old, in control of more than twenty-four newspapers and a readership of nearly 1.5 million.[11]

Bob Scripps was a reluctant newspaperman. As a teenager, he'd found journalism repugnant and devoted himself to poetry, art, and travel, often straining his relationship with E.W. After studying at Pomona College,[12] he finally consented to learning about publishing, and E.W. sent him east to apprentice at papers in Philadelphia and Cleveland.[13] He worked in a variety of roles within the family business but never stopped reading or writing poetry, often spending many hours alone with his books. Bob made frequent trips home to the family compound, which is where he met his wife, Margaret Culbertson. The historical record contains little about Nackey's mother, but one Scripps biographer described her as tall, brunette, and the daughter of a businessman from Pasadena who was a regular guest at Miramar.[14] Bob and Margaret were married in the spring of 1917 and immediately began juggling a fast-growing family with the high-profile, high-pressure world of newspaper publishing.

Nackey was the fourth of the couple's six children. (Her older brothers were Robert and Charles. Her older—and only—sister was Margaret, who, like their mother, went by Peggy. Her two younger brothers were Samuel and Edward.) The name on her birth certificate is Elizabeth Anne Scripps, but she was always called Nackey.[15] News of her birth on February 24, 1924, reached her famous grandfather off the coast of Panama, where he was traveling aboard his massive yacht, the *Ohio*, on one of the many ocean voyages he took during his retirement.

"Eight-and-a-half-pound girl born Sunday morning," the cablegram reported.

"Congratulations," E.W. replied a day later. "Boys are nuisances anyway."[16]

That summer, after sailing into the Chesapeake Bay, E.W. would meet his new granddaughter when her parents, who were in Baltimore for a newspaper conference, brought her to visit him at a hotel. "She is a rugged, healthy and good-natured baby," E.W. wrote in a letter. "To a marked degree, she resembles most of my own children when they were her age; the texture of her skin and the general form of her face are similar to a number of the Scripps babies I have known and dissimilar to a large number of other babies that I have seen and observed."[17]

Until she was about ten, Nackey's family spent part of each year in a big, white farmhouse in the woods of Ridgefield, Connecticut. The location put her father in reasonable proximity to New York and Washington DC, but it was rural enough to satisfy his desire for open spaces.[18] Although Nackey remembered her time there fondly, she always considered Miramar home. At the ranch, the Scripps children were paradoxically both sheltered and unsupervised. Their material needs were well met, and they were largely unaware of the concerns of the outside world. But the adults paid little attention to their daily exploits, leaving them to entertain themselves and mediate childhood squabbles.[19] Bob was consumed by the demands of the newspaper business and traveled often, sometimes alone and sometimes with Peggy by his side. Many of their trips attracted publicity, such as when Bob spoke at the League of Nations in 1926 as part of the first International Press Conference. Several years later, Peggy made a splash of her own when, while Bob conferred with a group of British publishers, she met the King and Queen of England.[20]

While Bob managed the papers, Peggy managed the household, organizing domestic workers and tending to the logistics of shuttling a half dozen children from East Coast to West Coast and back again. Hired help was a big part of growing up in the Scripps family. For a time, Nackey and her sister had to contend with a terrifying governess who would beat the girls every morning to punish them in advance for any mischief they might make during the day. (When the elder Peggy found out, she fired the woman immediately.) That governess was the exception, however, and Nackey had fond memories of just about everyone else employed on the ranch. Among her favorites was a carpenter named Roy who worked in a little toolshed near one of the bunkhouses. Decades later, she'd still remember the sign on his wall that read, "A good workman swears by his tools, not at them."[21]

The Scripps story is generally told through the lives and accomplishments of its men, but at least two women in the family were involved in newspaper management before Nackey. Both were part of the vast constellation of relatives she interacted with during her childhood. The first was her aunt Josephine Stedem Scripps. Josephine was married to E.W.'s oldest son, James, who died shortly after seizing control of seven papers and leaving the larger Scripps newspaper chain. (His departure was part of the same dispute that put Nackey's father in charge of the family business.) After James's death, E.W. attempted to regain control of those papers, but Josephine fought him in court. She eventually won and became the first woman to have a majority ownership of a modern newspaper chain. She ran the company—which she named the Scripps League—for ten years before turning it over to her sons.[22] After her retirement she continued to serve on the Scripps League's board while managing Fanita Ranch, a property adjacent to Miramar. It was there that Nackey and her sister—despite their mother's protests that such work was unladylike—would join Josephine's branch of the family on multiday cattle drives, getting their meals from a chuckwagon and curling up in sleeping bags at night.[23]

The other, and perhaps better-known, Scripps newspaperwoman was Ellen Browning Scripps, E.W.'s half sister, mentor, and business partner. Her career in newspapers started before his, when she joined another brother, James (not to be confused with E.W.'s son James), at the *Detroit Evening News*. She worked on the copy desk, helped keep the books, and wrote a daily column called "Miss Ellen's Miscellany." For fifteen years she put in long shifts in the newsroom and at night helped care for James's children—an arrangement that allowed her to save her income and invest it in the *Evening News*. A young E.W. joined the family in Detroit, where he too worked at the newspaper, first in circulation and later as city editor.[24] During the 1890s Ellen convinced him to move out west and launch a newspaper concern of his own. She loaned him the startup money for what would eventually become the Scripps-Howard newspaper chain and served as his business consultant for many decades.

The two settled in the area around San Diego, and Ellen soon earned a reputation as a generous philanthropist. By the 1920s her frugal habits and smart investments had made her rich, with a fortune estimated at $30 million. She spent her time and money advocating for women's rights and supporting the many entities in California that bear the Scripps name, including Scripps College and the Scripps Institute of Oceanography.[25] Ellen had no children of her own, but she adored her many young relations. For Nackey, the feeling was mutual. As a little girl, she loved visiting her great-aunt in La Jolla. There was a large basket of toys in the living room and, in Ellen's bedroom, a giant picture window looking out on the Pacific. "She was a very special lady," Nackey wrote many years later. "There are many who would say that if it were not for her, my grandfather, E. W. Scripps, would not have succeeded."[26]

Young Nackey was lanky and athletic and often wore her hair in the kind of sporty bob that was popular among girls and women at the time. She loved animals, especially horses; an old family movie shows her as a toddler astride a pony. She spent most of her time outside, riding through the Sierra Nevadas and attending horse shows and the occasional rodeo.[27] She and her older brother Bob were close, and some of her favorite memories involved helping him with agricul-

Family Business

tural experiments such as de-budding tomato plants and harvesting honey from the ranch's beehives.[28] Nackey attended a mix of public and private schools, eventually graduating from The Bishop's School, an all-girls Episcopal academy in La Jolla that Ellen and her half sister, Virginia, founded in the early 1900s.[29] As Nackey's artistic talent developed, she began to imagine a career as a medical illustrator. She left Miramar to study art at another all-girls institution founded by Ellen: Scripps College in Claremont, California. She wasn't always the best student, but she loved learning, especially about history, architecture, and music.[30]

During Nackey's childhood, the family newspaper chain expanded rapidly under the direction of Nackey's father and his business partner, Roy W. Howard. The two acquired new publications, including, in 1931, the *New York World*. It soon merged with the *New York Telegram* and became the *New York World-Telegram*, giving the company a sizeable footprint in an important media market.[31] Outside of work, Bob avoided social engagements whenever possible, preferring to spend time alone with his books. He drank heavily and spent long stretches of time aboard his yacht, the *Novia Del Mar*, sailing off the coast of Southern California.

It was there, a week after Nackey's fourteenth birthday in 1938, that he died of a throat hemorrhage at the age of forty-two. His sudden death rocked American journalism and made international news as questions arose about the future of the chain. Howard assumed command, assisted by editor in chief George B. Parker and by William W. Hawkins, a loyal and long-serving Scripps-Howard manager whom Nackey's mother would marry several years later.[32] Bob's death also marked a significant shift in Scripps family finances. Under a trust created by E.W., much of his fortune and assets passed to Bob's children. As was customary at the time, the boys received far more than the girls, but Nackey was still left with a generous lifetime income. The annual sum varied, but at one point in the late 1940s, it was estimated at $40,000 to $100,000—the equivalent of roughly $450,000 to $1.1 million in today's dollars.[33]

As she was entering her senior year at Scripps College, Nackey became engaged to her first husband, a tall, blond chemist with an entrepreneurial streak and a fondness for adventure. George Gallowhur grew up in an affluent East Coast family and attended the prestigious Hotchkiss School in Connecticut. He went on to Princeton and, while he was still an undergraduate, made national news when he sailed across the Atlantic in a fifty-foot cutter.[34] He and Nackey met through mutual acquaintances—they were third cousins—and eloped to Las Vegas in the fall of 1944. At forty, Gallowhur was twice her age. He'd achieved some fame thanks to the success of Skol, a popular suntan lotion he'd helped invent. He was also the founder and president of Gallowhur Chemical Corporation, which during World War II developed water purification systems, bug spray, and anti-mildew products for the army. His work drew the attention of *Time* magazine, which portrayed him as a patriotic scientist committed to the war effort. Gallowhur, the article proclaimed, was "the hero of a little business career as American as ice cream."[35]

In the years before he met Nackey, Gallowhur lived a double life, splitting his time between a farm in central Vermont and Manhattan's Turtle Bay. There, he was a regular presence in New York's closeted gay community. This portion of his life is documented in *The Gay Metropolis*, a sweeping history of gay life in America published in 1997 by journalist Charles Kaiser. Although Gallowhur passed for straight professionally, his friends in the city knew he quietly pursued relationships with younger men. Shortly before marrying Nackey, Gallowhur's heart was broken by one such companion—Otis Bigelow, then in the early years of a long career as an actor, playwright, and respected stage manager. He was serving in the Navy Reserve at the time, and Gallowhur had offered to buy him a ship and donate it to the Coast Guard, with the stipulation that Bigelow would serve as its captain. Bigelow found Gallowhur attractive, but he was in love with another man and declined.[36] It's unclear if Nackey was aware of this aspect of her fiancé's life, although she did spend time at his apartment in Turtle Bay during their marriage.

Family Business

Gallowhur owned a two-seater plane, and in October 1944 he used it to fly Nackey to Las Vegas, where they were married by a justice of the peace.[37] They left soon after on their honeymoon, with plans to visit Mexico for a mix of relaxation and business. On the way they stopped near Palm Springs, spurring breathless coverage in the local society pages. "Prominent couple now honeymooning at Desert Inn," one headline proclaimed.[38] They returned to the United States and moved to Gallowhur's farm in Reading, Vermont, a tiny town in the central part of the state, about twenty miles west of the New Hampshire border. A year later, they had a daughter. In keeping with Scripps family tradition, they named her Nackey.

The Gallowhurs' marriage would be short and unhappy. He spent long periods of time away, including a three-month stay in Florida. Despite Nackey's protests, he availed himself of her inheritance, spending $340,000 over the course of four years to cover expenses related to his business, renovate the farm, and buy a yacht called *Right Royal*. Nackey, by comparison, spent just $14,000 during that time. He also convinced Nackey to borrow $150,000 from her mother to invest in his chemical company, which he was trying to reshape for the postwar economy.[39]

Nackey was never a socialite, but after moving to Vermont, she did attend occasional dinners and other gatherings—including a party hosted by one of Gallowhur's classmates from Hotchkiss: an unconventional, ambitious newspaper publisher named William Loeb III.[40] Nearly two decades older than Nackey, Loeb was of average height, with a slightly round face and a mostly bald head. He was born in 1905 in Washington DC to Catharine and William Loeb Jr. His father, a stenographer by training, worked as Teddy Roosevelt's personal secretary and, after Roosevelt became president in 1901, took on a role similar to chief of staff. When the elder Loeb and his wife welcomed their only child, they picked the president and First Lady as the baby's godparents. After Roosevelt left the White House, the Loebs followed him to Long Island and settled in a home near the former president. The elder Loeb served as the customs collector for the Port of New York before going on to have a successful and lucrative business career. In 1930 he was included on a list of sixty-four men who ruled the United States.[41]

The younger Loeb's professional path was more eclectic. After Hotchkiss he attended Williams College in western Massachusetts, where he studied philosophy, joined the debate and shooting clubs, and dreamed of becoming a lawyer. That career plan ended in the wake of a contentious divorce from his first wife. During his final year at Williams, Loeb married a Smith College professor named Elizabeth Nagy and won acceptance to Harvard Law School. He enjoyed his legal studies, but his marriage soon became rocky. He had an affair, and Elizabeth accused him of violating the state's anti-adultery law. Facing the threat of arrest, Loeb had to drop out of Harvard and leave Massachusetts. The divorce between Nagy and Loeb was finalized in 1932, and Loeb began searching for another vocation. This phase of his life coincided with the Great Depression and the start of World War II. "Idealistic and troubled by what he saw happening in the world, Loeb, like many, grasped for answers," a documentary about his life explains. "He sought an identity separate from being William Loeb's son. At the same time, he took advantage of its privilege. Using his father's business connections, young Loeb looked for a means of financial independence."[42]

He worked as a salesman hocking rum and paint and tried to patent a few inventions, including self-lighting matches. He got involved in politics, too, but not the conservative kind he'd later become famous for advocating. In 1934 Loeb raised money for Upton Sinclair, an author and socialist running for governor of California. A few years later, the elder William Loeb died and Loeb took over management of the family's investments, a role that gave him access to financial capital. He'd been fascinated by newspapering since his law school days. In October 1941 he bought his first newspaper, the *St. Albans Messenger*, a daily with a circulation of four thousand in northwestern Vermont, where he started his tradition of front-page editorials. A year later he bought his second paper, the *Burlington Daily News*, one of several publications covering Vermont's largest city.[43]

Despite their age difference, Nackey and William had a lot in common when they met. They'd both grown up surrounded by powerful people, and they both believed independent newspapers were crucial for democracy. They were also both married—Nackey to Gallowhur and Loeb to his second wife, Eleanore McAllister, whom he'd wed in 1942. Still, Nackey admired what she would later call Loeb's "tremendous love affair with this country. He loved America deeply, and he loved the ideals that he thought represented America."[44] Nackey soon became a regular presence at the *Burlington Daily News*, sitting in on meetings and working briefly as a typesetter in the composing room.[45]

The circumstances of William Loeb's expansion into New Hampshire are fraught with personality clashes and financial complexities. The *Union Leader* traces its roots back to 1912, when Col. Frank Knox—a member of Teddy Roosevelt's Rough Riders and secretary of the navy under Franklin D. Roosevelt—launched the *Manchester Evening Leader* with the goal of supporting Teddy Roosevelt's Bull Moose party. Knox soon merged his paper with the *Manchester Daily Union* and ran the company until his death in 1944.[46] (Although Knox served a Democratic president, he was a longtime Republican and was the party's vice-presidential nominee in 1936.) His widow, Annie, had no desire to take over for her husband and, in 1946, agreed to sell the paper to Loeb, in part because of his father's connection to the first president Roosevelt. Loeb lacked the cash for such a big investment, so he recruited help from executives affiliated with Ridder Publications Inc., one of the many big publishing chains blossoming at the time.[47] That partnership was short-lived, and Loeb, seeking more control, convinced a new associate, Leonard Finder, to buy out the Ridders in 1947. The following year, they acquired the *New Hampshire Sunday News*, a fledgling paper founded by B. J. McQuaid and Blair Clark. The partnership between Loeb and Finder soured, and by 1949 Loeb had the resources to buy him out, a move that gave him total control of New Hampshire's only two statewide newspapers.[48]

McQuaid worked as one of the Loebs' top editors for many decades, and his son, Joe, would become one of Nackey's closest colleagues. Clark, meanwhile, went on to a long career in journalism and politics, serving as editor of *The Nation* magazine and as Democrat Eugene McCarthy's campaign manager in 1968. In an unpublished memoir, Clark documented many of his dealings with Loeb, recalling that Nackey often accompanied the publisher on trips to Manchester. They were both still married to other people at the time, so their frequent appearances together at the Manchester Country Club stirred gossip.

The couple's politics were another source of conversation among locals who were unaccustomed to such a vitriolic brand of conservatism. Loeb may have flirted with socialism as a young man, but he had since taken a hard right turn. This became apparent during New Hampshire's 1952 presidential primary. It was the first time the names of candidates, not delegates, would appear on ballots, so there was a lot of excitement among voters about the race. Further bolstering interest was an intense effort by establishment Republicans, led by New Hampshire governor Sherman Adams, to convince Dwight D. Eisenhower to seek the presidency. Conservatives, meanwhile, backed Robert Taft, an isolationist U.S. senator from Ohio. One of Taft's greatest champions was William Loeb. But the *Union Leader*'s support didn't help Taft; he finished second in the primary, eleven points behind Ike. The 1952 election shaped Loeb's reputation in another way, though, inspiring two of his most iconic political taunts. Soon after the new president took office, Loeb labeled Eisenhower "Dopey Dwight." Sherman Adams, who was serving as chief of staff, earned a moniker too: "Shermy Wormy."[49]

Nackey's worldview had always been conservative, which is no surprise given her California roots.[50] The state may be deep blue today, but that's a fairly recent development. In the years after World War II, California—especially the southern part where Nackey grew up and maintained many family ties—was the site of concentrated and often extreme anti-communist activism. Many historians point to the region as an incubator for the modern right-wing movement. Still, Clark was surprised when he learned of Nackey's connection to E. W. Scripps, a man known for his left-leaning politics. "Her views in no way resembled the progressive ones of her grandfather," Clark wrote in his unpublished

Family Business

memoir. "She enthusiastically embraced the arch-reactionary notions that Loeb trumpeted on the front page of the *Union Leader*."[51]

At the same time as Loeb's New Hampshire newspaper operations began to settle down, his personal life grew even more complicated. In 1948 he and his second wife had a daughter, Katherine Penelope Loeb.[52] Nackey, meanwhile, had left her husband's rural homestead and was living in Burlington's University Heights neighborhood, where Loeb was a frequent guest at her apartment.[53] As their relationship grew more serious, Loeb decided to introduce Nackey to his mother, who was spending the summer of 1949 in a house about four miles away from the Gallowhur farm. Over dinner at his mother's table one Friday night in August, Loeb began to describe his plans to divorce his second wife and marry Nackey.

A knock on the door interrupted the conversation. A local police chief was there to serve court papers to both William and Nackey, and he'd been sent by Gallowhur. A few days before, Nackey's husband had discovered love letters between his wife and Loeb that included, among other things, the date, time, and location of that evening's dinner. Enraged, Gallowhur sued Loeb for $150,000, accusing him of "alienation of affections" under an old Vermont law. He also started divorce proceedings against Nackey, alleging she had treated him with "intolerable severity." The police chief's arrival caused a commotion, and as soon as Nackey realized who was at the door, she snuck away to collect her daughter and hide at a neighbor's house. The chief demanded to know her whereabouts. Loeb refused to say where she'd gone, a decision that earned him a night in jail.[54]

Over the next few weeks, the tiny courthouse in Windsor County, Vermont, became a focal point for the national media as Nackey and Gallowhur sued and countersued. Nackey filed for divorce on August 15, 1949, outlining Gallowhur's spending habits and frequent absences from the farm. One local reporter covering the case dubbed it the "George Gallowhur–William Loeb–Mrs. Nacky [sic] Gallowhur divorce and alienation tangle."[55] The story was big enough to jump international borders. Ontario's *Windsor Star*, for instance, published the headline

"Hubby Faces Counter Suit. Wife Says Spouse Spent Her Money."[56] Nackey's health began to deteriorate from stress, and she developed hives, insomnia, and stomach problems.[57] That October, Gallowhur dropped his alienation of affections claim against Loeb and agreed to a divorce settlement. Nackey was awarded primary custody of their daughter plus the couple's 1948 Jeep. Gallowhur kept a Bentley, an older Jeep, and the yacht. He was also ordered to repay some of the money he'd spent.[58]

William Loeb remained married to his second wife for several more years and then obtained what was known at the time as a "Reno divorce." By moving to Nevada he was able to take advantage of a law that allowed even brand-new residents to quickly end their marriages, which he did in July 1952.[59] His legal troubles with the second Mrs. Loeb would continue, however, as the two fought over custody and child support for their daughter Penelope. (With the exception of a few brief visits, Loeb and Penelope remained estranged for the rest of his life.)[60] The day after a judge granted Loeb's divorce, he and Nackey married in a small church ceremony in Reno, attended by a few friends, Nackey's daughter, and other members of the Scripps family. Her sister Peggy was matron of honor. The best man was William Montague, general manager of the *Union Leader*.[61] When Nackey's mother realized her daughter was marrying a newspaperman like William Loeb, her response was brief and accurate: "Well," she said, "at least it won't be dull."[62]

"Rotten, Biased Journalism"   **3**

Instead of returning to the East Coast, the Loebs moved to a ranch outside of Reno, an arrangement that put Nackey closer to her family and, because it was the state where William Loeb obtained his divorce, simplified some of the legal troubles with his second wife.[1] They nicknamed their new home the Nevada Star and turned it into a remote headquarters for their newspaper business, using phones, telegrams, and mail to stay in touch with their employees and a growing network of politicians, journalists, and other powerful people.[2] Outside of work, they rode horses and went skiing. He served as a trustee at a Presbyterian-Congregationalist church nearby. Nackey taught Sunday school there and volunteered with the parent-teacher association at the local elementary school.[3] At home she took on increasingly ambitious art projects, including Fabergé eggs, pottery, and sculpture.[4]

Although there were some initial rumblings that the Loebs might enter the Nevada newspaper market, those plans never came to fruition. Their decision to operate their New England newspapers from the other side of the country was, for many, a headscratcher, but they made it work. To Nackey, the arrangement probably resembled the type of management she'd seen in her youth. The Scripps-Howard chain was based in Ohio, but her father, and before him her grandfather, had successfully run the business while spending long periods of time at Miramar. Despite living thousands of mile away from their properties, the Loebs were not absentee publishers; they made regular trips back east and were a common sight in their New Hampshire newsroom and in downtown Manchester—so common that, decades later, the owner of a deli near the *Union Leader*'s offices could still rattle off Loeb's standard lunch order: pea soup, a chopped ham sandwich, and coffee. (Nackey frequented the same deli, but the owner didn't mention if she had a favorite menu item.)[5]

Loeb was the public face of their newspaper operation, giving speeches to various conservative groups, serving on the board of the National Rifle Association, and, of course, writing inflammatory front-page editorials. Nackey worked informally behind the scenes. She had a keen sense of the publishing business and helped with hiring, handled the couple's correspondence, and consulted on matters both political and managerial.[6] "While I was married to him, not only did I take care of the kids and do this and that around the house, but I read the mail and we talked over the newspaper," she said in an interview many years later. "Most of the conversation was newspaper business and most of our friends were associated in one way or another with the newspaper."[7]

Nackey's role during this period in the *Union Leader*'s evolution is often overlooked, likely a function of both her introverted personality and prevailing gender norms. But as the *Nevada State Journal* once reported, Nackey played "as much a part in the newspaper's direction as [her husband]."[8] William Loeb was the subject of many profiles over the years; most included cameos from Nackey. In one, she answers the door for a visiting reporter and explains the map she drew of the ranch's riding trails. In others, she knits or does needlepoint while William Loeb fields questions. A *60 Minutes* segment shows her wordlessly firing a pistol at a backyard target while the narrator notes she's a far better shot than her husband.[9] She also appears in photos that illustrate the couple's rise to national prominence: shaking hands with President Nixon at a White House luncheon; smiling after William Loeb is presented with a media award by the Women's National Republican Club; greeting readers at various community events hosted by the *Union Leader*.[10]

Nackey embraced this arrangement, often saying she'd rather listen than speak, but she did occasionally step out of William Loeb's long shadow to interject her voice into the political debate. The first time

"Rotten, Biased Journalism"

this happened was during the summer of 1954 when the *New York World-Telegram*, a flagship of the Scripps-Howard chain, published stories criticizing Senator Joseph McCarthy's anti-communist efforts. McCarthy's sensational rise to prominence had occupied a significant place in the national consciousness for several years. By the mid-1950s, though, his Senate colleagues and many members of the public were losing patience with his high-profile and often-unfounded investigations into alleged communist sympathizers in the U.S. government. In a five-part series, Pulitzer Prize–winning reporter Frederick Woltman, a man *Time* magazine once dubbed the "No. 1 newspaper specialist on Reds,"[11] concluded that the senator was a "major liability to the cause of anti-communism," a phrase the *World-Telegram* used multiple times in headlines accompanying the series. Woltman argued that McCarthy had "brought distortion and confusion to the picture; introduced a rabble-rousing technique to the serious business of exposing the Communist conspiracy; distracted attention from the grave threat of Soviet aggression; driven a wedge into the Republican Party and immeasurably lowered the prestige of the Senate."[12]

The stories were reprinted throughout the Scripps-Howard chain, putting Woltman's reporting on breakfast tables and in living rooms across the country. McCarthy's critics had new fodder. His supporters—a shrinking group that included the Loebs—had a new focal point for their outrage. While average McCarthyites were limited to grousing with friends, or perhaps writing letters to their local papers, Nackey used her unique position to make a splash nearly as big as the Woltman series itself.

Her older brother Charles E. Scripps had taken over as chairman of the Scripps-Howard board the year before, and she sent him an angry telegram. The stories were "rotten, biased journalism," she complained, "which would make my grandfather, E. W. Scripps, who above all stood for integrity and fair play in the handling of news, turn in his grave in disgust and shame. For many months now, the Scripps papers have been carrying on a vicious campaign through slanted news reports and editorials to discredit Sen. McCarthy. . . . My name Scripps is on the masthead of every Scripps-Howard paper, and I want to make it clear beyond the slightest doubt that I abominate and loathe your anti-McCarthy stab in the back." She also predicted that the series would hurt the chain financially. "The American people are not fools, and they are just about fed up with slanted newspapers."[13]

The Loebs made sure Nackey's criticism became public, printing the telegram on the front page of the *Union Leader* on July 17, 1954, under the headline "Scripps Granddaughter Assails Anti-McCarthy Newspaper Series." They also sent copies to friends at other newspapers. Soon Nackey's complaint was national news. Wire services picked up the story, and in early August, so did several major magazines. Charles Scripps seems to have avoided public statements, but Roy Howard dismissed Nackey, telling *Time*, "Mrs. Loeb has no connection, direct or indirect, with the management of the concern. She has just the same right to send a telegram as my cook or anyone else."[14]

It's not unusual for siblings to quarrel over politics, but Nackey's decision to challenge her brother and his colleagues is notable because it marks her public debut in a right-leaning zeitgeist that would, in the following decades, coalesce into the conservative movement. Many of the things Nackey championed throughout her life, such as small government and a strong military, were standard fare for Republicans. But she also sometimes aligned herself with more strident conservatives by supporting measures—McCarthy's anti-communist crusades, for instance—that put ideology and political expediency ahead of fact.

Nackey once told an interviewer that she had always identified with the political right, and William Loeb "whetted" her opinions.[15] Beyond that she never said much about the roots of her worldview, although the timing and circumstances of her childhood likely played a role. She was born several years after women won the right to vote, so like many of her peers, she never connected with feminism. (Her great-aunt Ellen Browning Scripps was a prominent suffragist, but Nackey was young when she died, so it's unlikely the two ever discussed politics.) During the Great Depression, the Scripps fortune insulated her from the harsh economic conditions that made many desperate Americans embrace new government programs like Social Security and welfare.[16] Nackey's early adulthood unfolded at the dawn of the atomic age in a world grappling with "a political and intellectual climate of anxiety" in which the specters of communism and nuclear annihilation loomed large.[17] When the United States entered World War II, Nackey was seventeen years old, and at least two of her siblings were stationed in the Pacific theater. Her sister Peggy worked as a correspondent for the *Honolulu Star Bulletin*; her beloved older brother Bob shipped out as an army private just a few days after the attack on Pearl Harbor.[18] Both returned safely, but their involvement gave her a personal connection to the danger caused by global conflict. By the time atomic bombs dropped on Japan in the summer of 1945, Nackey was living in Vermont and pregnant with her first child.

Another formative experience that may have shaped Nackey's views about government relates to her taxes. At the same time as she was divorcing her first husband and becoming more deeply involved with Loeb and his newspapers, she was fighting in court to reduce the tax burden on her inheritance. In the late 1940s, Nackey sued the Scripps trust, claiming that the trustees were calculating taxes in a way that reduced payout to both the heirs and a fund set up by E. W. Scripps for the purchase of additional newspapers. The case was filed in Ohio (Scripps-Howard was based in Cincinnati), and Nackey fought all the way to the state's supreme court, which ruled against her in December 1950.[19] Her disdain for taxes would shape her politics and her business decisions for the rest of her life.

As a native of Southern California, Nackey didn't have to look far to find other people who were terrified of communists and frustrated with federal overreach. Many historians consider the region a cradle of modern right-wing politics. "Its conservative movement was the nucleus of a broader conservative matrix evolving in the Sunbelt and the West that eventually propelled assertive and unapologetic conservatives to national prominence," historian Lisa McGirr argues.[20] White, upper-class women played a crucial role in advancing the conservative cause in California and beyond; they organized chapters of the ultraconservative John Birch Society, opened conservative bookstores, and testified at school board meetings against what they viewed as liberal educational policies.[21] There's no evidence that Nackey was part of this kind of grassroots activism. She wasn't really one for social clubs ("not a joiner," her oldest daughter explained). She also had a much bigger platform with which to advance her cause. While other right-wing women of her generation brewed coffee for John Birchers, knocked on doors, and mimeographed pamphlets, Nackey worked alongside her husband to turn the *Union Leader* into a loud and enduring voice in the national political arena.

To understand the role the Loebs played in the rise of the conservative movement, it's important to know about the nascent right-wing media ecosystem that took shape during the mid-twentieth century. At the same time as mainstream journalism was becoming more profession-alized, more corporate, and more focused on achieving objectivity, a parallel network of conservative outlets was gaining popularity and helping to connect like-minded Americans. As historian Nicole Hem-mer explains: "By the late 1950s, 'conservative media' had emerged as a meaningful concept with a coherent set of key figures. Sharing national reach and overlapping coverage, enterprises like the *Manion Forum*, *National Review*, *Human Events*, and Regnery Publishing were for many people the center of conservatism in America. . . . But audi-ences did more than just listen and read. They saw these broadcasters, editors, publishers, and writers as authorities on conservatism. When questions arose about how best to shape their own beliefs, readers and audiences turned to media activists for answers."[22]

The leaders of these right-wing outlets also popularized the idea of liberal media bias—something Nackey complained about often throughout her life, starting with her critique of the Scripps-Howard chain's coverage of McCarthy. Before the emergence of conservative media, most Americans, including those on the political right, viewed the news as reasonably fair or even biased against liberal policies like

"Rotten, Biased Journalism"

the New Deal. That began to change during the 1950s and 1960s as ring-wing publishers built platforms to push back against prevailing media narratives. "Just like motherhood and apple pie," one political scientist writes, "it made perfect sense to conservatives that the media was not an ally to their cause. And since it was against their cause, the media was un-American."[23]

The Loebs certainly weren't the only publishers to use a local newspaper to spread conservative ideas, but the growing significance of New Hampshire's first-in-the-nation presidential primary cemented them as important members of the national right-wing media. The Granite State's place in the election calendar is rooted in Yankee frugality. During the early 1900s, New Hampshire embraced the tenets of the progressive movement and began holding primaries to give voters, as opposed to party elites, more power. In 1916 lawmakers scheduled the state's first presidential primary for the second Tuesday in March, when municipal buildings would already be open for town meeting day.[24] The decision saved money and put New Hampshire at the front of the voting line; and despite frequent challenges, the state has held its place ever since. The primary was fairly low key, however, until 1952, when voters were able, for the first time, to choose candidates instead of delegates.[25]

Over the next several decades, both the primary and the *Union Leader* became increasingly important in national politics, blending together to create an electoral mythology that gets retold every four years. Winning New Hampshire is not a golden ticket to the White House, but doing well can help a candidate maintain or gain momentum. Although a campaign's financial resources and the influence of party elites still matter, New Hampshire is ripe with opportunities to upset conventional wisdom through better-than-expected vote tallies, improved public perception, or both. The inverse is true too. Many would-be presidents have had their hopes dashed by subpar performances or because they failed to spend enough time shaking hands and kissing babies. "No one," historian Stuart Sprague wrote, "has ever been overprepared for New Hampshire." The electorate is wildly unpredictable too. As Sprague notes, "Voters' preferences in the Granite State defy simplistic analysis; more crow has been eaten by political pundits trying to explain away untoward primary results here than in any other state."[26]

The New Hampshire primary also has its critics; the argument over its prized place is longstanding. Detractors say the state is too white and too rural to properly vet national candidates. Supporters contend that New Hampshire's small size makes it the perfect arena for retail politics, allowing even underdog candidates to reach voters. Despite this enduring debate, the state still has a big role in how American presidential elections are perceived, as political scientists David Moore and Andrew Smith explain: "Candidates, political leaders and—most importantly—the press all believe that the New Hampshire primary is monumentally important."[27]

Even without the nation's first primary, New Hampshire's political culture would be fascinating. The population is small—about 1.36 million today and a little over 500,000 during the 1950s—and many residents believe in limited government in terms of taxes, regulations, and bureaucracy. When it comes to elected officials, though, New Hampshire is *huge*. Its massive citizen legislature is one of the largest parliamentary bodies in the English-speaking world, with four hundred house members and two dozen senators. Governors have notoriously limited power; they serve two-year terms and need approval from a five-member executive council on state contracts, long-term infrastructure planning, and many staff appointments. Outside the capital, home rule is the general philosophy, with even the tiniest towns controlling local budgets, roads, schools, and law enforcement. The result is a personality-heavy pageant of civic life ripe with opportunities for people like William and Nackey Loeb to exert influence.

Although the Loebs lived and voted in Nevada, William Loeb quickly became a larger-than-life figure in New Hampshire and beyond.[28] During elections the *Union Leader* had more impact on the outcomes of local races than it did in presidential contests.[29] But its influence extended beyond vote totals. Potential candidates sometimes didn't run at all out of fear of Loeb's wrath or doubt that they could win because he was backing another campaign. As the *Columbia Journalism Review* once explained, "Most office-seekers hope for Loeb's support, or at least his neutrality. His help can save them from obscurity; his opposition leads almost surely to vilification."[30] Loeb's critics often accused him of bias, complaining that his friends received positive coverage, while foes were more likely to receive negative press.[31] Loeb disagreed, citing the editorial label borne by all of his front-page missives as evidence that he separated opinion from news.

It was, however, indisputable that Loeb's editorials drove the policy conversation. He popularized what's known as "the pledge," a vow against new, broad-based taxes that candidates for most of the state's elected offices still take today. The practice has its critics, but it's endured long enough to make New Hampshire one of a handful of states without a sales or income tax. Sometimes his crusades succeeded; sometimes they didn't. Loeb supported the construction of both a nuclear power plant and an oil refinery on the state's seacoast. The power plant continues to operate today. The refinery plan was abandoned after intense protests by residents in neighboring towns. Loeb also tackled social issues. When, for instance, a club for gay students at the University of New Hampshire won official recognition in the mid-1970s, Loeb protested in an editorial headlined "Boot Out the Pansies."[32] (The students were eventually allowed to organize the club, and a modern version still exists at the university today.) As one journalist observed several years after Loeb's death, his "editorials over time amounted to a first rough draft for much of the New Right movement."[33]

When Loeb arrived in New Hampshire, the local press corps wasn't sure what to make of him. "New Hampshire folk have not been witness to his type of journalism since the days when newspapers were primarily the organs for political parties," a columnist for the *Nashua Telegraph*, a competing paper about twenty miles south of Manchester, observed in 1954. The columnist disliked Loeb's politics but was impressed with how fast his newspapers were growing. He also described him as a rather likeable guy: "unfailingly courteous, a good public speaker, altogether a witty and charming person to be with."[34]

Opinions about Loeb's personal attributes differed, but his New Hampshire newspapers were indeed prospering. The Loebs invested heavily in distributing the *Union Leader* to even the most rural corners of the state, giving them unparalleled control over the local media and, by extension, coverage of the primary.[35] By 1966 the *Union Leader* had the highest circulation of any New Hampshire–based paper, distributing 53,800 copies each day in a state with 194,000 households. There was still plenty of competition, however, albeit from publications with smaller coverage areas. The state's other eight dailies had a combined circulation of 82,000. Three major Boston newspapers—the *Globe*, the *Herald*, and the *Record American*—also were distributed in New Hampshire, although they were most popular near the southern border, with a collective Granite State circulation hovering around 58,700 daily.[36]

Running—and growing—the company was a round-the-clock endeavor for the Loebs. The *Union Leader* and the *New Hampshire Sunday News* were financially strong, but the rest of the operation was more precarious. The *Burlington Daily News* went out of business in 1961, and attempts to expand the company were unsuccessful. In the late 1950s, the Loebs started a new paper, the *Journal*, in Haverhill, Massachusetts, a mill city just south of the New Hampshire border. The venture soon devolved into a years-long legal fight between William Loeb and the rival *Haverhill Gazette*, with both sides alleging antitrust violations. The case ended in the spring of 1965, when Loeb agreed to pay the owners of the *Gazette* a $1.25 million settlement. The next month he closed the *Journal*.[37] That same year, the Loebs bought another paper—the *Connecticut Sunday Herald* in Bridgeport—but their foray into that state was brief, and the *Herald* soon folded.[38] Sometimes Nackey wondered if the newspapers should have been included in their wedding vows. "The days started with the first telephone call to dictate an editorial and ended with [William Loeb] plowing through piles of papers for more grist for the editorial mill," she wrote many years later. "Vacation

"Rotten, Biased Journalism"

luggage consisted of two bags of reading material for every one bag of clothes. . . . It was this way because he loved it."[39]

As their New Hampshire newspapers grew in both circulation and reputation, the Loebs' domestic life got busier too. Their daughter, Edith, was born in the mid-1950s. Around the same time, they bought a second home on the East Coast that put them closer to their newspapers and, every four years, the political action. Reno, with its horse trails, wide open landscape, and sagebrush, remained home; but the family spent almost half the year at their thirty-room Tudor mansion in Prides Crossing, an exclusive Boston suburb on the Massachusetts coast, about an hour's drive from Manchester. The house and grounds were massive, with a full-scale security system, a heated outdoor pool, tennis courts, and space for backyard target practice.[40] The mansion soon became a common destination for the politically ambitious. Declared candidates and those just starting to mull a presidential run were frequent guests, as were political operatives who came calling on behalf of their bosses.

During this time, Nackey once again weighed in publicly on national politics when she drew an editorial cartoon opposing federally mandated integration of the public high school in Little Rock, Arkansas. In 1954 the U.S. Supreme Court ruled in *Brown v. Board of Education of Topeka* that racially segregated public schools are unconstitutional. Change came slowly in most parts of the South, and many schools remained segregated. The situation attracted intense national attention in the fall of 1957, when nine African American teenagers attempted to attend Little Rock's Central High School. White residents were outraged, and Arkansas governor Orval Faubus dispatched the National Guard to bar the students from entering the school. A federal court ordered Faubus to withdraw his troops, and the teenagers—who became known as the Little Rock Nine—attended classes for a few hours one morning in late September. City police officers removed them when a crowd of more than a thousand angry, white protestors grew big enough to threaten the students' safety. President Dwight D. Eisenhower called the protests "disgraceful" and sent in members of the 101st Airborne Division, a decision that turned Little Rock into "*the* central symbolic event" in 1950s racial politics.[41]

The federal troops escorted the Little Rock Nine into class on September 25, 1957. That day, William Loeb editorialized against the integration order, arguing it violated the rights of individual states and moved the federal government closer to dictatorship. "You can't teach mutual respect and liking between black and white at the end of a bayonet," he wrote. "This newspaper abhors and detests un-American and un-Christian discrimination against Negroes, which takes place in the North as well as the South. But you cannot force whites to associate with blacks by the use of court decrees. . . . Progress was being made—too slowly, but definitely in the right direction—toward mutual self-respect between black and white. Then came the segregation decision by Eisenhower's Supreme Court. This attempt to use force . . . stopped peaceful evolution of racial harmony right in its tracks."[42] (Many people disagreed with Loeb's characterization of life in the segregated South, where African Americans lived under constant threat of violence, a truth that was reinforced when members of the crowd outside of Central High threatened to lynch a sixteen-year-old black girl.)[43]

Nackey used her artistic skills to bolster her husband's argument by drawing an editorial cartoon called "Brotherhood by Bayonet!" that depicted armed soldiers shoving two little girls—one white, one black—together in front of a schoolhouse. The image appeared on the front page of the next day's *Union Leader*. A caption underneath the image reads, "Start loving each other. That's a court order!" It was a simple line drawing, but the cartoon quickly attracted the attention of segregationist groups and, to use a modern term, went viral. A copy of the *Union Leader* edition that included the cartoon made its way to the Arkansas governor, and a photo of Faubus holding up the front page was distributed on the international wires. Nackey's cartoon was later reprinted in newsletters, passed out at rallies, and turned into

"Rotten, Biased Journalism"

a bumper sticker that continued to appear in the South well into the next decade.[44]

Pivotal in the cartoon's widespread distribution was the White Citizens' Council, a white supremacist group that arose in response to the *Brown* decision. In 1955, in an effort to communicate with its sixty thousand members, it launched a newspaper called *Citizens' Council* that eventually evolved into a magazine called simply *The Citizen*, which reprinted Nackey's cartoon. The magazine had a circulation of about three thousand and branded itself as a publication for educated segregationists, distancing itself "from the extreme racial hatred of the Ku Klux Klan, yet cloaked in its own brand of respectable and 'intellectual' racism." A typical issue would include summaries of crimes committed by African Americans, various unflattering and sometimes untrue stories about Martin Luther King Jr., and reports of bogus, pseudoscientific studies that purported to show that integrated schools were damaging to African American children. Federal overreach, states' rights, and religious arguments stating that God had, for unknowable reasons, made nonwhites inferior were also standard fare. Largely absent was any coverage of Klan violence or police brutality against marginalized communities.[45]

The Loebs' ties to the White Citizens' Council persisted for decades. William Loeb was a featured speaker at the their leadership training in New Orleans in 1972, and *The Citizen* printed a lengthy profile of Loeb the same year, under the headline "Yankee Publisher Friend to South." It was packaged with Nackey's cartoon and a caption that read "Dramatic drawing by Mrs. William Loeb . . . graphically projects the still relevant message of Little Rock."[46] When Loeb died in 1981, *The Citizen* devoted the cover (and many pages) of its winter issue to his legacy, calling him a "giant" in American journalism and once again reprinting Nackey's "Brotherhood by Bayonet!" cartoon. A couple of years later, *The Citizen*'s editors again lauded the *Union Leader*, reprinting a story about Nackey that had originally appeared in a different magazine. In a thank-you note to the editor, Nackey marveled at the long relationship she'd had with *The Citizen* and reported that the *Union Leader* was doing well. "We seem to be confounding a lot of people who hoped we would simply fade into the woodwork," she wrote. "Unfortunately for them, we are thriving."[47]

It might seem odd that the Loebs, who owned newspapers in New England and lived primarily in Nevada, would link themselves so closely to a southern cause. But the Loebs viewed themselves as part of a national fight. Their unusual living arrangement gave them access to conservative power brokers around the country and turned the *Union Leader* into an ideological conduit that transcended geography. William Loeb saw supporting segregationists as a strategic move that might benefit conservatives. While many right-wing politicians were trying to sidestep the topic of race or frame it as only an issue of states' rights, Loeb wondered if conservative Republicans should double down on their support for segregation in an effort to drive away African Americans and other moderates. In a letter to an acquaintance in the South, he suggested that the GOP "become the white man's party." African Americans might then vote for Democrats, but, he predicted, white voters would become Republicans, something he said would help in the next election because "white people, thank God, are still in the majority."[48]

Each new primary brought a fresh opportunity for the Loebs to raise their profile. The 1956 race was a sleeper. Eisenhower won easily both in New Hampshire and nationally, although the *Union Leader* did editorialize against an attempt to remove then vice president Richard Nixon from the Republican ticket. That was the beginning of an on-again, off-again relationship between the Loebs and Nixon. They supported him in 1960, helping him win the New Hampshire primary and the nomination, although he eventually lost to John F. Kennedy. But when Nixon ran again in 1964, he didn't win the *Union Leader*'s endorsement. Instead, the Loebs joined the many other right-wing activists who propelled Arizona senator Barry Goldwater to national prominence and helped him secure the Republican presidential nomination.

"Rotten, Biased Journalism"

The *Union Leader* enthusiastically supported Goldwater, unleashing some of its most infamous editorials on his main primary challenger, Nelson Rockefeller—a divorced and remarried man whom Loeb labeled, among other things, a "wife swapper." The irony of the thrice-wed Loeb attacking Rockefeller wasn't lost on the national press; when asked, Loeb argued that his personal life didn't matter because he wasn't seeking public office.[49] (Neither Goldwater nor Rockefeller won New Hampshire in 1964. That victory went to Henry Cabot Lodge, who pulled in 35 percent of the vote.)[50] During the campaign, Nackey met Goldwater several times. She liked him but worried the country might not be ready to elect someone with such strident right-wing ideals. "He was a very interesting person," she said. "He was the beginning. He sort of broke through as far as the conservative voice was concerned."[51]

Goldwater lost the general election. Four years later, in 1968, Nixon ran again, winning the *Union Leader*'s endorsement, the New Hampshire primary, and the White House. But during his first term, he fell out of favor with the Loebs because of his administration's diplomatic outreach to China. In protest, the *Union Leader* endorsed Ohio congressman John Ashbrook in the 1972 GOP primary, but he earned only 10 percent of the vote. The Loebs couldn't bring themselves to endorse Democrat George McGovern in the general election that year. Instead, William Loeb famously advised readers to hold their noses while voting for Nixon. Nackey was equally displeased; years later, she called him a "sham conservative."[52]

Attempting to topple a sitting president wasn't the only thing that drew attention to the *Union Leader* in 1972. That election cycle made William Loeb even more notorious, thanks to a now-infamous feud with presidential candidate Edmund Muskie. Muskie, a senator from Maine, was that year's Democratic frontrunner and the recipient of a volley of attacks from the *Union Leader*. Loeb dubbed him "Moscow Muskie" and reprinted a *Newsweek* editorial claiming that his wife, Jane, smoked and told dirty jokes. Two weeks before the primary, the paper published a letter accusing Muskie of using the slur "Canuck" to describe French-Canadians. (Months later, the letter was revealed to be a hoax planted by the Nixon campaign, but Loeb maintained he had no idea it was fake.)[53] Muskie retaliated, giving an emotional speech from the back of a flatbed truck parked outside the *Union Leader*'s building. Some journalists reported he'd cried, although others who were closer to the truck later disputed that account. It had been snowing lightly that day, and they said it was melting flakes, not tears, that made his cheeks appear wet. That detail got lost in the hubbub, though, as the senator's campaign collapsed and William Loeb became known as the man who made Muskie cry.[54] Years later, Nackey would call Muskie "the greatest public relations man [the *Union Leader*] has ever had."[55]

The Muskie incident became legend. But something far more significant in the evolution of the modern political landscape had happened quietly four years earlier when, as the 1968 election cycle opened, a young man named Patrick Buchanan arrived at Prides Crossing in the middle of a snowstorm. Buchanan, a Columbia School of Journalism graduate with a flair for pithy, biting prose, was already making a name for himself as a conservative columnist. Although the Loebs had never met him, they knew his name well. The *Union Leader* reprinted many of the editorials he wrote while on the staff at the *Globe-Democrat* in St. Louis, and the Loebs admired his writing style and strong conservative philosophy. Buchanan knew the Loebs' reputation, too, and had read about how hard they had worked on behalf of Goldwater four years before. He had recently joined Richard Nixon's presidential campaign and knew that the Loebs' support would help his new boss, so he volunteered for a fact-finding mission to gauge their feelings.

Heavy snow was falling when Buchanan arrived in the Loebs' neighborhood. The cab driver got disoriented and threatened to drop him off on the side of the road. Then Buchanan saw a car with a "Stand Up for Alabama" slogan above its license plate. "This would be it right here," he told the cabbie, and he scurried to the front door where William and Nackey were waiting. They talked politics, of course, and Nixon would win the *Union Leader*'s endorsement and the presidency in 1968. But what Buchanan remembers most about meeting the Loebs is their hospitality. Staying at their house, he said, made him feel like "a kid

"Rotten, Biased Journalism"

coming home from boarding school." They offered him sherry, and when he went upstairs to his guest room, he found milk and cookies by the bed. "They could not have been more gracious." After Nixon's victory, Buchanan joined his administration as a speechwriter and advisor. To commemorate his new job, the Loebs sent him a gift: a black briefcase engraved with the words "Pat Buchanan, White House."[56]

Surviving for a Reason   **4**

The week before Christmas 1977, a Jeep Wagoneer skidded out on a highway near Reno. The causes of the accident—black ice and a faulty tire bolt—were mundane, but the people involved made the crash national news.[1] William and Nackey Loeb had spent the evening dining with their minister and were returning home to their ranch. It was a short trip and one they'd made many times before, but on that night it ended in disaster. A few minutes after 8:00 p.m., the Jeep flipped over an embankment and fell thirty feet, crushing the roof and trapping Nackey under the dashboard. Neither she nor William Loeb lost consciousness, and as they waited for help, he heard her repeat, "I can't breathe. I can't breathe." When paramedics arrived to cut them from the wreckage, Loeb, confused and worried, demanded they take care of Nackey first.

William Loeb suffered cuts and bruises. Nackey's condition was far more dire. Her back, ribs, and breastbone were broken, and her lungs were so heavily damaged that she needed a respirator to breathe. The pain medication made her hallucinate. At first she thought the hospital staff was trying to kill her with scissors. Then she became convinced they were running a drug ring from the nurses' station. Unable to talk, she scribbled panicked notes to her family as they tried to calm her. Although she had a bit of feeling in one foot, it soon became clear that she would never walk again—devastating news to anyone but especially to someone as athletic as Nackey. Well-wishers called by the dozens, sending seventy-two telegrams and fifty-six flower bouquets. Christmastime that year was grim, with Nackey learning to breathe on her own again and William giving frequent updates to the national press. He injected a bit of normalcy into the situation when he paused during one interview to assure a reporter that he and Nackey still planned to support Ronald Reagan in the 1980 GOP primary.[2]

Nackey returned to the East Coast on a private jet in early January, arriving at Logan Airport to a press scrum waiting on the tarmac. A photo of her strapped to a stretcher and wrapped in a plaid blanket went out on the national wires. She spent the next few months in rehab, learning how to transfer herself in and out of her wheelchair and take care of various physical needs. The process was grueling and often brought her to tears. Even simple tasks like brushing her teeth or putting on stockings pushed her to the brink of exhaustion. One day, when Nackey was especially tired and frustrated, a nurse gave her an ultimatum: "You only have two choices. You can either lie down and spend the rest of your life in bed . . . or you can do the lousy exercises, push yourself to make yourself improve." Nackey picked the second option.[3]

In April she checked herself out of rehab, went home to Prides Crossing, and began to determine what parts of her old life she could resume and what she had to let go. "She never asked 'why me,'" said her eldest daughter, Nackey Scagliotti. "Self-pity was never part of her persona, even during the toughest times."[4] Physically demanding forms of art like sculpture and pottery were too difficult, but she began to explore new mediums and became fascinated by tempera painting—a tricky, multistep process that she mastered. Skiing and horseback riding were no longer possible for her, but she eventually relearned to bowl and skeet shoot from her chair.[5] She also resumed fly-fishing, one of the Loebs' favorite pastimes. In the summer after the accident, they traveled to the Canadian wilderness, where Nackey used an off-road wheelchair to access a camp on the Kedgwick River. When they returned, a photo of her sitting in her wheelchair and hoisting a twelve-pound, thirty-inch salmon in the air appeared in the *Union Leader* alongside a column William Loeb wrote about the trip.

There had been other challenges for the Loebs that year too. In Jan-

Surviving for a Reason

uary the *Vermont Sunday News* ceased publication, leaving the Loebs with only two newspapers: the *Union Leader* and the *St. Albans Messenger* in Vermont. A few months later, Nackey's mother died after a series of strokes. Most troubling, though, was William Loeb's declining health. In the early 1970s he'd been treated for prostate cancer; although they'd hoped for the best, the Loebs weren't surprised when it returned shortly after Nackey's accident. William's prognosis was poor, and they began making plans for Nackey to take over the publishing business after his death. In 1979 they converted 75 percent of their newspaper company's stock into a trust under Nackey's control and formally installed her as co-president and co-publisher. "After I die," William Loeb said at the time, "I want the paper to be run by people who share the same philosophy that I do, that of public service."[6]

The Loebs knew that projecting strength was key to maintaining the *Union Leader*'s political influence. They also worried that competing newspapers in New Hampshire or Massachusetts might see William Loeb's illness as an opportunity to expand, so they kept his cancer a secret. As his health declined during the late 1970s, Nackey took on more and more of the daily tasks, eventually writing many of the letters he signed.[7] Nackey had never been meek, but her long, difficult recovery helped her connect with her inner strength and self-confidence. "I became much more of a person after the accident," she said. "I had a sureness of what I wanted to do, an ability to handle things that I don't know if I could have before. . . . I didn't have the tools of walking, but I had other tools."[8] In some ways, she felt like she'd escaped death for a reason. "I figured that there's a purpose to my surviving," she said. "Darn if I know what it is, but I better stick around and find out."[9] William Loeb began to reconsider her abilities too. "He finally realized that I was much stronger, and that I was able to handle things like the paper."[10]

During the summer of 1981, the Loebs sold the *St. Albans Messenger*. William's health worsened, and he lingered in the hospital for weeks. When Nackey visited, she wasn't sure if he knew she was there. "The last six months . . . watching him lose ground and not be able to do anything was rough," she once told an interviewer. "We did so much together. Our whole life was together."[11] William Loeb died at the age of seventy-five on Sunday, September 13, 1981, thirty-five years after buying the New Hampshire newspapers that made him famous and twenty-nine years after marrying Nackey. When she called the *Union Leader* offices to report the news of his death, she did not cry or stammer. "Well," she said over the phone, "it's happened."[12]

Although newspapering was (and still is) an overwhelmingly male profession, it's not uncommon for leadership responsibilities to pass to a publisher's widow. Perhaps the most well-known example of this is Katharine Graham, who assumed control of the *Washington Post* after her husband's sudden death in 1963. Like Nackey, Graham had grown up in the newspaper business, but unlike Nackey, she had very little practical experience running a newspaper when she took over. Nackey had worked side-by-side with William for decades, but she still had doubts about her new role.[13] She was fifty-eight years old and, despite her many behind-the-scenes efforts, had never held a traditional job. As she later said in an interview, she spent much of the year after her husband's death wondering, "Can I handle it? Can I run a meeting and tell people they can't have this or that?"[14] Nackey usually came to the paper's downtown Manchester building once or twice a week. There was no wheelchair ramp, so it was a struggle at first for her to get inside. "They had to haul me up the stairs," she said. "That trims you down to size."[15] She had a ramp installed, figured out how to squeeze her chair behind her late husband's mammoth desk, and began to write frequent front-page editorials and even more frequent memos.

The *Union Leader* was unusual for its role in national politics, but operations were fairly typical for a newspaper at the time. During the day, reporters tracked down stories, advertising representatives made sales calls, and managers gathered for meetings. At night, editors hustled toward deadline as the presses began to rumble. The opinion section was led by Jim Finnegan, a prolific editorial writer who shared the Loebs' zeal for conservative rhetoric. (The *Union Leader* didn't have an editorial board. Instead, Nackey, Finnegan, and other top editors discussed endorsements and issues informally.) Finnegan also curated the op-ed pages, offering a buffet of columns from local conservatives and national right-wing mainstays like Patrick Buchanan, William F. Buckley, and Phyllis Schlafly.[16] The news sections, meanwhile, focused heavily on life in the Granite State. The front page on November 3, 1981, for instance, included a couple of updates on municipal elections and a three-column photo of a Manchester police officer corralling a three-hundred-pound escaped pig that had run loose through several neighborhoods the night before. High school sports were always a big deal. So were wedding announcements, profiles of local business owners, and assorted features about small-town life.

Nackey said often how grateful she was to have inherited a team of good managers, but that group lost a key member in 1982 when the paper's editor in chief, Paul H. Tracy, died suddenly. His death left Nackey mourning the loss of a man she respected while needing to quickly pick his successor. She chose Joseph McQuaid, the lanky and often mustached son of B. J. McQuaid, one of the founders of the *Sunday News* and Loeb's longtime colleague. Like Nackey, the younger McQuaid had grown up in the newspaper business and understood that the *Union Leader* needed to serve both the local community and a national political audience. He was in his early thirties and had already worked at the paper for nearly twenty years, starting as a part-time sports and office boy before climbing the editorial ranks.[17] Still, McQuaid—who the *Columbia Journalism Review* once described as "brash"—needed mentoring, and it often came from Nackey.[18] "I could be rather hotheaded at times and demanding of the staff," he said. "I would get motherly notes from Mrs. Loeb which, in essence, said, 'take it down a notch.'"[19]

Not everyone working for the *Union Leader* agreed with Nackey's politics, but by most accounts, she was collegial and attentive, often sending handwritten notes of praise for good news stories, smart business decisions, and other jobs well done. She weighed in on the mundane frictions of office life, too, soothing tensions around an outdated heating system and refereeing arguments over production schedules. But she had her limits. Once, she refused to intervene in a long-festering dispute between smokers and nonsmokers, declaring in a bulletin board memo that she wouldn't touch that particular issue "with a 10-foot pole."[20] Many of the people who worked closely with Nackey remember how much she emphasized collaboration, especially during her first few years as publisher. "From her perspective," McQuaid said, "we should all be working together and not claiming territories."

When Nackey first started as publisher, there was a lot of scuttlebutt about the new boss around the *Union Leader*'s offices; most of the staff was willing to give Nackey a chance, in part because of her connection to the Scripps empire.[21] One exception was a longtime reporter named R. Warren Pease, who grew frustrated with what he viewed as the paper's milder approach to state political coverage. About six months after Nackey took over, Pease left in a public huff. "There have been no new issues since Mr. Loeb died. There have been no new crusades," he told the *Boston Globe*, fueling another round of stories surmising that the once-powerful *Union Leader* had gone soft.[22]

If Pease had stuck around a little longer, he would have seen that he was mistaken. Nackey had every intention of mounting regular political crusades, something she began to demonstrate in April 1982. New Hampshire's gubernatorial race was heating up, and the incumbent Democrat, Governor Hugh Gallen, had been a favorite rhetorical punching bag for William Loeb. Nackey was eager to see him replaced, but the field of challengers wasn't to her liking. She called them "the sorriest bunch of birds ever to crowd a coop" and promised to pay close attention to the race. "This newspaper has no intention of letting ANY candidate get away with . . . wishy washy behavior."[23] She spent the summer criticizing Gallen, blaming him for a budget deficit, labeling him as pro-tax, and calling him a "flop" as governor.[24]

Her efforts yielded mixed results. Gallen lost in November, but not to the Republican the *Union Leader* preferred. The paper had endorsed the state senate president, Bob Monier, but he was defeated in the primary by John Sununu, who went on to serve as New Hampshire's governor for six years and later became chief of staff for President George H. W. Bush. Still, Gallen's supporters were furious, especially when they realized he had performed poorly in regions with the highest *Union Leader* circulation. Nackey, Gallen's campaign manager complained, had gone "absolutely all out to torpedo" the governor.[25] The *Union Leader's* treatment of Gallen was comparable to what the paper had unleashed on Democrats in past campaigns; but the surprise seemed to be focused on the fact that Nackey was capable of such tactics.

Nackey soon demonstrated that she could influence more than elections, which was a good thing, at least for a ten-year-old boy named Doug and his pet ferret, Electron. Ferrets weren't allowed as pets in New Hampshire, and Nackey was outraged when she heard that state game wardens had ordered Doug's family to euthanize Electron. She devoted her May 29, 1983, front-page editorial to the matter, accusing the New Hampshire Fish and Game Department of governmental overreach and demanding that the ferret be saved. "It is not the law that is an idiot, but rather it is the law enforcer acting out of stupidity or lack of compassion or both," she wrote. "We suggest that the governor should issue a stay of execution, the Legislature should immediately pass a bill guaranteeing the safety of one small brown pet ferret and the Fish and Game Department should get back to more important duties." Public outrage grew and the governor signed an executive order protecting Electron, although ferret ownership wouldn't be permitted by New Hampshire law for another decade.[26]

Still, a narrative persisted that Nackey was somehow less capable and less powerful than her husband—a function, most likely, of perceptions about both her disability and her gender. McQuaid fielded constant questions from the national media about her level of involvement and long-term plans for the paper. Eventually, he decided to write a column about his new boss for *Editor & Publisher*, a popular national magazine about the newspaper industry. He portrayed Nackey as a competent manager presiding over a company with increasing circulation and plans for future growth. He pointed out that the White House was paying attention to her, too, citing her visit with Reagan in Boston. He wrote the column without telling Nackey he was doing it, explaining to the magazine's editor, "If I'd asked her in advance, I have a hunch she would have said, 'Oh, fiddlesticks, I haven't done all that much!'"[27]

Another of Nackey's champions was Meldrim Thomson, a fellow archconservative who served as New Hampshire's governor for most of the 1970s and ran a sugar house that was a favorite stop for Republican presidential candidates. (His maple syrup was so good that even some devoted Democrats would stop by to grab a pint.) He and the Loebs were kindred spirits in both their ideology and their rhetorical tactics. When Thomson left the governor's office in 1979, he became a regular columnist for the *Union Leader*.[28] After William Loeb's death, Thomson and his wife, Gale, stayed in frequent contact with Nackey, exchanging letters and dropping by to visit, sometimes by themselves and sometimes with an ambitious politician in tow.

Thomson thought many of the profiles written about Nackey were dismissive of her abilities, so he interviewed her himself for *Conservative Digest*. Like McQuaid, he portrayed her as a competent newspaperwoman, but he devoted most of the article to showcasing her right-wing credentials. "Despite her confinement to a wheelchair, she picked up the reins of authority in the firm and capable hands of the superb horsewoman that she had been, and led the great statewide New Hampshire newspapers to a new era of prosperity and independent conservatism." He described her as "a quiet, almost shy, gentle lady with a ready wit and steel-trap mind. . . . This lovely, courageous and inspiring lady . . . works diligently every day at making America's heritage meaningful for every inhabitant in this land of the free. If she were a liberal, she would be one of the most famous American women in the world."[29]

At the same time Nackey and her supporters were building her public persona, she was rebuilding her life to reflect the realities of both her injuries and her new job as publisher. "Being in a wheelchair, you can

Surviving for a Reason

get around, you can get things done, but you have to limit yourself," she said. "You have to plan the effort, the energy that you put into things and say, 'I'm not able to do all the things that I want to, so I have to pick out the important ones.'"[30] One thing she decided wasn't worth her time was the hour-long commute to and from Prides Crossing. She closed out her husband's estate, put the mansion up for sale, and reluctantly resigned from the Massachusetts Rifle Association because she would be too far away to make use of its shooting range.[31] In early 1983 she moved to a horse farm a short drive away from the *Union Leader*.

Her older daughter, Nackey Scagliotti, had married an architect, and Nackey collaborated with him to design a simple, wheelchair-accessible home with a breathtaking view of foothills and fields. Her younger daughter, Edie, lived at one end of the house with her husband and, eventually, their two small children.[32] On the other side of an open-concept kitchen, dining, and living area, Nackey kept her room. It wasn't fancy, but it had everything she needed: a hospital bed, a TV, and plenty of space to work on newspaper business and artistic pursuits. She rigged a couple of accessible desks by laying hollow doors across filing cabinets, and set up a small table where she'd help her grandkids with crafts or play round after round of the card game Uno.[33] There was also space to host newspaper executives who visited for meetings and the politicians who sometimes came calling.

"It is a wonderful, crazy household," Nackey wrote to a friend, noting that, in addition to her human family members, she had five dogs and two cats there to keep her company.[34] She missed the Nevada Star, but travel was too difficult and time-consuming, especially given her new responsibilities.[35] She continued to manage the ranch from afar for several years and sometimes missed the open space and the smell of sagebrush, but she eventually sold her Nevada property. "Sorry to see that part of my life go by," she wrote to a friend. "But times and circumstances change and right now I'm so bloody busy back here between the newspapers and the primaries and, of course, the grandchildren, that I could not take the time to get out there anyway."[36]

Sometimes Nackey felt like she never had enough time to get everything done. In the colder months, especially during frantic election years, she'd dream of her summer fishing trips to the Canadian wilderness, when she'd roll her off-road wheelchair down the riverbanks to cast line after line. "You don't have to make any decisions at all, beyond the choice of flies," she wrote in a letter to a friend. "We go out fishing early in the morning before the sun is hot on the river and then we fish in the evening until dark, so the rest of the day is spent loafing, just sitting on the porch and watching the river roll by."[37]

Her life in New Hampshire was hectic, but it was the best living arrangement she'd had. Nackey hadn't been unhappy during her marriage to William Loeb or her childhood at Miramar, but the life she built in New Hampshire gave her newfound independence. For the first time, she and she alone could decide how each day would unfold.[38] Large windows gave Nackey a view of the changing seasons, busy birdfeeders, and the horse barn where Edie was starting a riding business. When the weather was good, she'd tour the property in a golf cart she nicknamed her "freedom buggy." Inside the house, she stayed fit with what she called her upside-down bicycle, a contraption she designed that allowed her to lay on her back and peddle with her hands while straps moved her legs to increase circulation.[39]

Over the years, Nackey received advice, moral support, and comradery through a newsletter for people with spinal cord injuries published by a California woman named Sue Owen. *The Bumblebee: An Exchange of Progress* launched in 1974 and continued until the mid-1990s, offering paraplegics the kind of first-hand experiences and practical tips that were difficult to find in the days before online support groups. Owen had been paralyzed in an accident in 1963, and she became an advocate for people with disabilities, contributing to rehab journals and a book on biofeedback therapy. The two women corresponded often, and the relationship was an ongoing bright spot in Nackey's life. Like Nackey, Owen had worked alongside her husband for many years, although their family business was a scientific lab, not a newspaper company. They also shared a knack for problem-solving when it came to the everyday challenges of living with a disability.[40]

Surviving for a Reason

Another key component of Nackey's new life was her wheelchair van, the Foxy Lady. It made daily logistics much easier, but she also liked that it resembled the vehicle in *Ironside*, a cop show featuring a detective who had been paralyzed in a shooting.[41] Her van had hand controls, so she could drive it if necessary, but she rarely did, preferring to ride in the back. On days when she came to the office, her secretary would drive to the farm, park her own car in the driveway, and use the van to take Nackey into Manchester. For night appointments, Nackey's driver was usually the *Union Leader*'s head of security.[42]

At the newspaper, she worked in an office she inherited from William Loeb, and for the first few years it remained largely unchanged.[43] The décor was dingy and out-of-date. His desk—a stocky, brown behemoth—was difficult for her to use, and because of the wheelchair, she could reach only a third of the surface. Nackey never complained, but her staff decided she should work in brighter, more accessible quarters. The day before Christmas 1985, McQuaid arrived at her house to take her to the *Union Leader* where, he said, a surprise was waiting. When she entered her office, she saw that it was transformed. A rug covered the linoleum floor, curtains hung from the windows, the old gray filing cabinets were gone, and in the place of William Loeb's desk was an expansive L-shaped table that was compatible with her chair. And on the wall: a painting of flowering fields and a mountain range that reminded her of the view from her farm. "It will be a lovely office," she wrote to a friend. "I suspect I will be spending more time there and create more headaches for the people who made the whole thing possible."[44]

Even today there's very little data on the number of journalists or media owners who have serious physical disabilities, but it's safe to say they're fairly rare. Someone like Nackey with a high public profile and a willingness to talk openly about her paraplegia drew immediate attention. She spoke often to advocacy groups in New Hampshire. In 1983 she helped a local chapter of the National Association of the Physically

Handicapped kick off National Employ the Handicapped Week, giving a speech that urged local businesses to hire people with disabilities. "Someone who is handicapped may not have as much physical energy," she said. "But he or she knows how to use the powers of concentration to the utmost. That ability to concentrate comes from long hours in therapy, when a person must try and try again."[45] She wrote editorials echoing similar themes. "A job is truly appreciated by the handicapped for it allows them to be a productive part of the world around them, to be accepted, to be needed, and to be rewarded for their efforts,"[46] she argued in one. In another: "The disabled know what work is, and they are willing to face it. A lot of temporarily able don't have that qualification. We call them temporarily able with reason. Everyone, including the employer, could at any time join the disabled. Hiring the handicapped is a risk worth taking."[47] Encouraging local businesses to hire people with disabilities was a common refrain for Nackey, and she sometimes pushed her editors to pursue stories about companies that had done so.[48] The *Union Leader* also printed a weekly column for readers with disabilities and their families, called "What About the Handicapped." It included information about support groups, social services, and other resources.

Although she was open about the limitations she faced because of the time and energy required to stay healthy, Nackey presented herself in the pages of her newspaper as an active person with a full life. Regular readers saw a feature story about her accessible house, photos of her shaking hands at community events, and dispatches about her latest fishing trip or painting class. She also supported efforts encouraging people with disabilities to lead active lives. Once, she editorialized in favor of creating wheelchair-accessible wilderness trails in northern New Hampshire. In another editorial, she chastised conservative commentator William F. Buckley for criticizing a blind man's attempt to sail across the Atlantic. Bad weather forced the man, Jim Dickson, to abandon his voyage, and Buckley used his misfortune as fodder for a syndicated column decrying risk-taking by people with disabilities. "If you cannot see the water and the skies, why are you going on a sailboat

Surviving for a Reason

to begin with?" he wrote. "The beginning of wisdom in respect to the handicapped is to recognize that they are handicapped. To treat them as though they are not handicapped is to deny reality. Let them do what they can do, but it's profane to suppose that a cripple can run, a deaf man hear or a blind man see."[49]

Dickson, who worked for a national organization that promoted sports and recreation opportunities for people with disabilities, quickly amassed a large contingent of supporters, including Nackey. "The world is a little better for what this one man tried to do," she wrote in an editorial, adding:

> Jim Dickson's attempt was no ego trip, nor was it ventured in order to attract pity for a blind man. Bill Buckley says that it is not normal for a blind man to sail solo, but it is also not normal for a man to be blind. In that regard, Jim Dickson has served the disabled well. When the temporarily able read that a disabled has risen above his disability, those who are "normal" must say, "Yes, there are those who are blind and they deserve not just sympathy, but they deserve our acceptance and our respect." The disabled have two choices in life: either go back to bed and stay there until they die, or accept life's challenges and do the best they can, in spite of the limitations. Bill Buckley should never underestimate the power of the disabled.[50]

Nackey's advocacy stopped, though, when it came to federal rules and regulations aimed at expanding public accommodation for people with disabilities. Shortly after she became publisher, President Reagan appointed her to the Architectural and Transportation Barriers Compliance Board, a federal agency created in 1973 to ensure that government buildings are accessible. She resigned after attending her first meeting in Washington DC, telling Reagan she was too busy to serve. "Either I would have to fail in my responsibility here at the paper, or else not give the required amount of time to the position as a member of [the board]."[51] Nackey was indeed entirely occupied by her newspaper, but she also disliked the idea of helping to craft more government regulations. "I somehow feel like a traitor," she wrote in a letter to Buchanan in 1984. "The very idea of my being associated with those in Washington who created the bureaucracy we all have to put up with bothers me."[52]

She also opposed the Americans with Disabilities Act (ADA), a landmark 1990 law that bans discrimination based on disability. The act is widely credited with improving the daily lives of millions of Americans by making things like wheelchair ramps, elevators, and curb cuts commonplace. Because of the act, people with disabilities have better—although still imperfect—access to employment, public transportation, schools, community spaces, and recreational facilities. To Nackey, though, mandating these things was an example of governmental overreach akin to federal troops arriving in Little Rock or New Hampshire Fish and Game wardens trying to snatch away a little kid's ferret. While Congress was debating the ADA, she wrote an editorial calling it a "bad bill for the disabled," arguing that it would create an "us-against-them situation between the disabled and the temporarily able."[53]

People with disabilities don't all ascribe to the same worldview, of course; one recent Pew Research Center study found that the ideological distribution of Americans who self-identify as disabled is similar to that of the overall electorate.[54] But the disability rights movement does often overlap with progressive causes. As one advocate explains, "Modern liberalism is concerned with issues of equality of opportunity and full participation for the marginalized, and it views societal discrimination as something that can be addressed through government initiatives. In that sense, disability rights and modern liberalism share a common goal: the pursuit of policies that—typically through funding and regulation—improve equality of opportunity."[55] As a conservative, Nackey saw things differently. The aims of the ADA were "commendable," she wrote, but she argued that it was wrong for business owners and taxpayers to be forced to support the cost of accommodating people with disabilities. "There is a misconception abroad in the land today that fairness is somehow the natural right of every individual, even though reality shows that life is not fair. . . . Fairness is something we

Surviving for a Reason

should celebrate when it comes our way. It's not something we should automatically expect as our inalienable right."[56]

Nackey's relationship with the disability rights movement is perhaps one of the most illuminating examples of her version of conservatism: Life, as she wrote in her anti-ADA editorial, is not fair, and it's not the responsibility of the state to make it otherwise. To her, government intervention, even the kind that might help her, was usually part of the problem, not the solution. This was an argument she would make over and over again and one that drove both her activism and her newspaper's editorial view.

Needle, Not Sword   5

During the summer of 1984, the Democratic Party made history when presidential nominee Walter Mondale picked Geraldine Ferraro as his running mate. For the first time, a woman would appear on a major party's ticket, a development that kicked into overdrive a long-simmering debate about women's roles in society. Supporters saw Ferraro as a symbol of progress toward gender parity and proudly wore heart-shaped campaign buttons with her face above the slogan "America's 1st Woman Vice Pres." Critics, meanwhile, accused Mondale of pandering to female voters. The 1984 presidential election was also Nackey's first as publisher. She had plenty to say about Ferraro, and none of it was good. In one editorial she called Mondale's choice "chickenhearted."[1] In another, she predicted that selecting Ferraro would "prove to be one of the WORST POLITICAL DECISIONS in American history."[2]

Many of Nackey's criticisms were similar to those she lobbed at male candidates over the years: She argued that Ferraro, a congress-woman from Queens, had a voting record that was far too liberal and that she lacked foreign policy experience. "We aren't thrilled with the thought of her sitting across the table from Soviet slave masters."[3] (While harsh, the *Union Leader*'s treatment of Ferraro was far more dignified than what some other news outlets published. A columnist for the *Denver Post*, for instance, said Ferraro had "nicer legs than any previous vice-presidential candidate" and wondered if she would be the first vice president to enter a wet T-shirt contest.)[4] But mostly, Nackey was incensed by the emphasis the Mondale campaign was putting on

Ferraro's gender. "It is just as immoral to promote someone simply because she is a woman as it is to discriminate just because she is a woman," Nackey said in an interview at the time. "It is especially so if that woman is chosen for a position that could possibly put her in the presidential chair."[5]

This would be one of many times when Nackey clashed with the progressive social trends that swept the country during her two decades as publisher. Although the history of female activism usually focuses on liberal causes, right-wing women like Nackey have also left their mark on American politics. Their work has been, in many ways, crucial to creating and advancing the modern conservative movement. In the years after World War II, conservative women—most of them white and affluent—framed their activism as a feminine crusade to protect the traditional American family from communism and other threats. Historian Michelle Nickerson describes these women as "housewife populists" who "cultivated an activist role for themselves as the defenders of the community."[6] During the Red Scare, they supported tactics like those used by Senator Joseph McCarthy. During efforts to integrate public schools in the South, they lobbied their local governments to uphold Jim Crow era policies.[7] During the 1964 presidential election, they were instrumental in Goldwater's rise to national prominence. And during the final few decades of the twentieth century, they played a significant role in the rise of the New Right, winning an internal battle within the GOP that continues to influence the party today.

In this pivotal struggle, socially conservative women prevailed over "Republican feminists," a label given to moderate members who supported the Equal Rights Amendment and, in some cases, access to legal abortion. As historian Catherine Rymph explains, "Conflicts between feminists and anti-feminists were an important part of the process by which the Republican Party remade itself in the 1970s and 1980s. . . . Each offered different women's political agendas, different models of how women could be politically effective, different visions of their party, and, indeed, different models of Republican womanhood."[8]

Needle, Not Sword

During the early years of this struggle, Nackey was still working mostly behind the scenes on newspaper business, but she was firmly in the anti-feminist camp. The Loebs aligned themselves with its most iconic figure: Phyllis Schlafly, a lawyer, author, and activist best known for her successful campaign against the Equal Rights Amendment. The Loebs and Schlafly weren't close friends, but they occasionally crossed paths at political events such as a Women's National Republican Club luncheon in the spring of 1977. William Loeb and Schlafly were among the award recipients that year; Nackey was at her husband's side as usual.[9] The Loebs also endorsed Schlafly's efforts to push the GOP to the right. When Schlafly ran for president of the National Federation of Republican Women in 1967, William Loeb quietly raised money to support her campaign. (Schlafly lost to a more moderate opponent, but her candidacy raised her public profile.)[10] Later, after Nackey became publisher, she, like Schlafly, would rail against the ERA, abortion, and the other social issues that helped invigorate the conservative movement at the time.

Nackey's chief tool for advancing her worldview was her front-page editorials, a feature central to the *Union Leader*'s brand that evolved to reflect both Nackey's personality and her position as a woman in the male-dominated arena of political commentary. At least once a week, readers would see a column in which Nackey laid out conservative arguments laced with God, family, folksy humor, and her vision of a free society. During her tenure, Nackey wrote roughly 1,650 editorials, totaling more than half a million words. That's an average of 86 editorials during each of the nineteen years she led the paper. (William Loeb, by comparison, averaged 171 editorials during each of his thirty-five years as publisher, for a total of more than 6,000.)[11] Nackey was one of several people writing regular front-page editorials for the *Union Leader*. (The others were, primarily, editorial page editor Jim Finnegan and Joe McQuaid.) What distinguished Nackey's work was its chatty tone. Her photo and signature also accompanied each editorial, helping to create a feeling of intimacy with her audience. Within a few years of her move to New Hampshire, she was a recognizable figure. "I can think of no greater compliment than when I am traveling around the shopping center to have people stop me to chat for a few minutes," she once wrote in a letter to a friend. "It slows up the shopping, but it is well worthwhile."[12]

Her earliest columns were short and focused on local drunk driving laws, William Loeb's legacy, and just before Columbus Day 1981, the importance of welcoming tourists visiting from out of state.[13] Soon she was writing more and more often, tackling a mix of subjects that reflected the *Union Leader*'s role as both a local newspaper and part of the national conservative media ecosystem. Nackey was far more comfortable with painting and drawing than with writing, but she eventually embraced the process, scribbling down thoughts before dictating drafts to a secretary or, later, typing them into a word processor or computer.[14] Serendipity played a role in her choice of topics too. She once told a longtime reader that she wrote mostly "by guess and by gosh, depending on the amount of time that I have and how angry I get."[15] She also drew occasional cartoons that appeared on the *Union Leader*'s front page. Some were whimsical sketches marking major holidays or highlighting New Hampshire's outdoor scenery; others tackled serious issues like abortion.

Inflammatory editorials had been William Loeb's main calling card, so comparisons between his work and hers were incessant. Nackey explained repeatedly that although she had a different voice and style, she shared her late husband's archconservative views. "Somebody once said he used a sword and I used a needle," she said in an interview. "But we were both aiming for the same target."[16] His often-rambling disquisitions were spiked with capital letters, unflattering nicknames, and sweeping hyperbole. At first Nackey sometimes mimicked his approach, such as when she dubbed New Hampshire governor Hugh Gallen "Hollywood Hugh" to emphasize her argument that he was out of touch with voters.[17] But she soon developed a style of her own that echoed the themes of housewife populism and anti-feminism that had come to define conservative womanhood.

Needle, Not Sword

To her, big taxes and big government were bad. Communism was a many-tendrilled threat to all she held dear. Permissive attitudes toward birth control, homosexuality, and gender roles jeopardized the sanctity of the American family. Feminists were bad. Gay and lesbian people—whom she called "sodomites" and likened to pedophiles—were worse.[18] Her approach to foreign policy was generally hawkish, and like many conservatives, she was wary of the United Nations, worrying that it would rob the United States of its sovereignty. Her suspicion of governmental overreach and communist meddling ran deep, so deep that she was sometimes willing to consider outlandish rumors. Once, for instance, she surmised in an editorial that the reason the pandas at the National Zoo had not reproduced was that the Chinese secretly had them neutered before giving them to the United States.[19] (The pandas eventually had several cubs, although none survived.)

Nackey's editorials, like Nackey, were unpretentious and ideologically unwavering. Her prose wasn't always elegant and her arguments often lacked nuance, but her work resonated with rank-and-file readers in New Hampshire and beyond. Also remarkable is how consistent her rhetoric remained over time. As social norms evolved, Nackey held firm. For nearly two decades, she churned out an eclectic stream of editorials that mixed the personal and the political in unexpected ways.[20] She wrote about her favorite pets and her least-favorite politicians, her grandchildren and American exceptionalism, the beauty of New Hampshire's wilderness and the threat of nuclear war. Her work was light on statistics, heavy on sass, and laced with nods to literature, pop culture, and Americana. Take, for instance, a piece she wrote in the fall of 1983, shortly after the sudden death of Rocky, one of her beloved bulldogs. The New Hampshire primary was just a few months away, so she could have devoted her column to any number of campaign issues. Instead, she decided to explore the human-animal bond through the lens of anti-communism. A city in China had just banned dogs, claiming that they were a nuisance and lacked social value. Nackey took issue with the new policy and in response wrote a long tribute to Rocky that concluded: "Do dogs have social value? We knew Rocky so we know the answer to that. . . . He taught us how to live a little better and he made us better. He taught us that joy should never be lost in the pressures of our days and that happiness should never be hidden. We see more clearly that love given freely is love returned. Rocky knew that secret, one that people so often forget. We are better for having known him. Of no social value? Not likely."[21]

Community, home, and family were common themes in Nackey's writing; she worried often that America's youth were ill-equipped to face geopolitical challenges. "We have cheated this generation of its faith in God . . . of much of its patriotism, its love of country, of my country, right or wrong," she wrote in 1987. "The flag is simply a pretty decoration. The principles on which the Constitution is based have little relation to teenagers' lives."[22] Another time, when she was troubled by a statistic about suicide rates among teenagers, she invited local high school students to share whatever was on their minds. "We would sincerely like to know more about who you are and where you are going. . . . We adults have too many opinions about what you should be—and too little knowledge of what you really are."[23] Kids wrote in by the dozen, and she continued to regularly ask local teens for their opinions on various issues. "The myth that elders won't listen to you is just a myth," she wrote. "We will listen."[24] She found opportunities to praise local kids too. When, for instance, some teenagers protested a proposed skateboard ban, Nackey applauded them for challenging unnecessary regulations, writing that "danger cannot be eliminated by passing laws."[25]

Nackey focused mostly on the serious issues of her day, but some of her writing reflects her corny sense of humor. During the summer of 1983, she started "The Great NH Cat Contest," asking readers to "tell us in 100 words or less, what makes your cat the cat's meow. And you must enclose a photo of the feline, preferably in black and white."[26] (Two years later, dog owners were invited to participate in a similar contest.) For Valentine's Day in 1985, she wrote a poem for

Needle, Not Sword

subscribers, proclaiming in the final stanza, "SO FOR EVERYONE AT THE UNION LEADER / OUR VALENTINE IS YOU, DEAR READER."[27] Ronald Reagan was also treated to a poem on the occasion of his seventy-sixth birthday when Nackey opened an editorial with "Commies are Red / The budget is blue / But Nancy is sweet / And so are you."[28]

Some loyal readers lamented the change in the *Union Leader*'s editorial tone. "When you read [William] Loeb over your cornflakes, he stayed with you," one Republican activist told the *Columbia Journalism Review* in 1983. "Now, you read the paper and you may forget what it said by the time you get to your office."[29] Others preferred Nackey's chattier voice and appreciated that her editorials tended to be shorter than her husband's. One early and enduring fan of her work was Joseph Wershba, one of the original producers of the CBS show *60 Minutes*. He first met Nackey in the early 1970s while he was filming a segment on the *Union Leader*, and he wrote her frequently after she became publisher. He often lamented her conservative tendencies—"When you laid all that sinning . . . [on] the Democrats, you lost me girl!"— but he encouraged her to keep writing.[30] "You haven't lost the Bill Loeb touch," he said. "I always suspected you invented it anyway."[31] A few months before the 1988 primary, he complimented her on her columns about the various candidates and urged her to keep them coming: "Go [at] it, girl!"[32]

Nackey's rhetorical techniques—and her position in the home of the first-in-the-nation presidential primary—helped her stand out in a cacophony of mostly male voices. Female publishers were extremely rare in Nackey's day. (In 1981, the year she became publisher, women represented roughly a quarter of a typical newspaper's staff but tended to be concentrated in clerical jobs. Management, meanwhile, was almost entirely male, with women holding 6.5 percent of the top positions.[33] By 2000, the year after Nackey retired, just 8 percent of U.S. papers with circulations over eighty-five thousand had female publishers.)[34] Even more unusual than Nackey's management position, though, was the prominent role she played in crafting the *Union Lead-*

er's editorial message. Even today, opinion writing and commentary are mostly male pursuits. Of the ninety-four named winners in the editorial writing category during the first hundred years of the Pulitzer Prizes, ten are women, and only two—Hazel Brannon Smith and Meg Greenfield—predated Nackey's time as publisher.[35] Although women's voices are becoming more common in civic discourse, opinion journalism and political commentary are a long way from gender parity. For instance, a 2014 study found that men represent the vast majority of U.S. newspapers' editorial board members and op-ed columnists.[36] On television, meanwhile, Sunday morning political shows also skew male, with one analysis finding that women represented just 27 percent of guests during 2015.[37] Talk radio reflects similar demographics, with only thirteen women appearing on a 2016 list of the top one hundred hosts.[38]

During Nackey's lifetime, female voices—not to mention female media owners—were even more rare, especially in conservative circles. Although Nackey was not a feminist, she still brought a female gaze to her writing. On at least two occasions, she encouraged readers to get breast cancer screenings.[39] And in a 1988 editorial, she argued for more awareness of domestic violence: "Neighbors have got to stop treating the noises from next door as just another spat, the concern of husband and wife alone," she wrote. "Police should treat a family fight as seriously as they do a barroom brawl."[40] But most of her rhetoric about gender reflected her right-wing, anti-feminist ideology. Her opposition to what she dismissed as "women's lib" was a common theme that remained stagnant despite the many ways the lives of American women changed during her time as publisher.

Like many far-right female activists, Nackey opposed the Equal Rights Amendment. She said repeatedly that she supported equal pay but thought the ERA was the wrong way to get it, arguing that it would be better to enforce existing antidiscrimination laws. She also disputed that another piece of sweeping federal legislation was necessary. "Let's admit it," she wrote in a 1983 editorial, "women in America have a pretty good deal. Unlike much of the world, we don't play the role of beasts of burden. We aren't considered the property of men. We have, when deserved, men's respect, and we have men's protection. . . . We are convinced that the ERA would ruin the deal for sure."[41]

Both major political parties drew Nackey's ire for, in her mind, paying too much attention to feminism. Ahead of the 1988 election, for instance, she chided the GOP for focusing on "women's issues," accusing the party of pandering to "a noisy and radical few who, we suspect, actually resent being women."[42] In 1993 she was outraged at President Bill Clinton's efforts to appoint more female cabinet members. In an editorial headlined "I Am an Angry Woman," she echoed her criticism of the Mondale campaign from a decade before. The Clinton administration, she wrote, was "demanding special positions for women." In that same 1993 editorial, she advocated for a return to more traditional gender roles. "There was a time, pre-women's lib, when it was an accepted fact that women were different from men. . . . Now housewife has become a dirty word and the hand that rocks the cradle has pushed down the doors of the board room."[43]

Nackey's strident anti-feminism helped her build influence in the conservative movement, but it also frustrated some of her readers and, as the years passed, her employees. In 1991, after Nackey summarized her views on gender in a profile for *Yankee Magazine*, many *Union Leader* staffers were upset—so upset that it prompted Nackey to respond with a staff memo. She reiterated her support of equal pay and equal access to most jobs, but she also said: "There are some duties that women simply cannot do as well as men, and I am talking about such things as hauling freight or pushing shovels. There are some places, such as men's shower rooms, where I don't think the presence of a woman reporter is as socially productive as a [man] reporter's presence would be. There are also, on some occasions, limits on a woman's time, especially when she is a wife and a mother and having to do two jobs at once, and I frankly suspect that few men would be capable of such a workload."[44]

Nackey worked for the most part in an analog world but employed techniques that would eventually become common in the blogosphere.[45] She curated bits and pieces of information from wire stories, television shows, and newsletters, often interspersing them with quotes from the many ordinary people who wrote her letters or called her on the phone. Her editorials also served as launchpads for civic engagement. She regularly printed contact information for local elected officials and activist groups—a crucial service in the years before Google—and suggested ways for readers to get involved with right-wing causes. In 1985, for instance, she promoted a petition against a tax on vending machine snacks.[46] A few years later, the *Union Leader* sponsored an anti-flag-burning petition that garnered more than twenty-one thousand signatures.[47] Another time, when the New Hampshire legislature was considering putting limits on ownership of semiautomatic weapons, Nackey suggested gun owners attend a hearing on the bill to help lawmakers understand that semiautomatics "are not just the ugly gun depicted by the anti-gun lobby. Semi-automatics include small guns carried in the purse for protection, hunting guns . . . and other legitimate guns used by those who enjoy the challenge of competitive target shooting."[48]

Although the issues Nackey addressed changed over the years, the core of her conservative ideology never wavered. One example of her commitment is her relentless campaign against a holiday honoring Martin Luther King Jr. Like many conservatives, Nackey believed King sympathized with communists and therefore did not deserve a national holiday. She reminded readers of this at least once a year. "We feel sorry for those who have chosen as their idol a man who associated with Communists and whose support by Communists gives blacks a sorry champion indeed," she wrote in early 1986, around the same time the first national Martin Luther King Day was celebrated. "Perhaps when information still officially suppressed finally comes out America will be able to know the whole story."[49] (Numerous documents related to government surveillance of King have been released in the years since Nackey wrote this editorial.

Needle, Not Sword

None of them have revealed evidence that King was a communist.[50] During his life, King often said that "communism and Christianity are fundamentally incompatible."[51])

The New Hampshire legislature created Civil Rights Day in 1993, but that did little to quiet a growing number of residents advocating for a King holiday.[52] Nackey, meanwhile, continued to editorialize against Martin Luther King Day, drawing increasingly intense criticism from people who thought her opposition was wrongheaded and racist. In 1996 she received some support, although not the kind she wanted. That year, Richard Barrett, the leader of the Mississippi-based Nationalist Movement, traveled to New Hampshire and held a small demonstration on the state house lawn to congratulate the state for refusing to declare a King holiday.[53] Nackey protested in an editorial. "We are not white supremacists" she wrote. "As a state, we are supportive of civil rights, but feel that they should not be applied to one race, nor should the hero figurehead for them be one individual. . . . Racists have every right to speak their piece, but they have no right to defame New Hampshire by characterizing us as participants in their cause."[54] (It's unclear how or if Nackey drew a distinction between this group and the White Citizens' Council, the white supremacist organization with which the Loebs aligned themselves for so many years.) It would take another four years for New Hampshire to declare the third Monday in January Martin Luther King Jr. Day, making it the last state in the nation to do so.

Despite Nackey's many efforts to shape the political debate locally and nationally, it's difficult to measure the impact of her work. The presidential hopefuls she endorsed in the primary didn't usually win in the general election; Reagan's reelection campaign is the only exception. And the *Union Leader*'s favored candidates for local office had mixed success. As for public policy, New Hampshire's political ethos still embraces low taxes and limited regulations—two things Nackey advocated for throughout her career—but the state is also fairly liberal when it comes to social issues such as gay rights and access to legal abortion.

Nackey's work may have yielded mixed success in terms of election outcomes and public policies, but her ability to reach like-minded Americans was a different story. Nackey was a master of audience cultivation. Throughout her career, she'd work relentlessly to get the *Union Leader*—and her unique editorial voice—in front of new readers in New Hampshire and beyond.

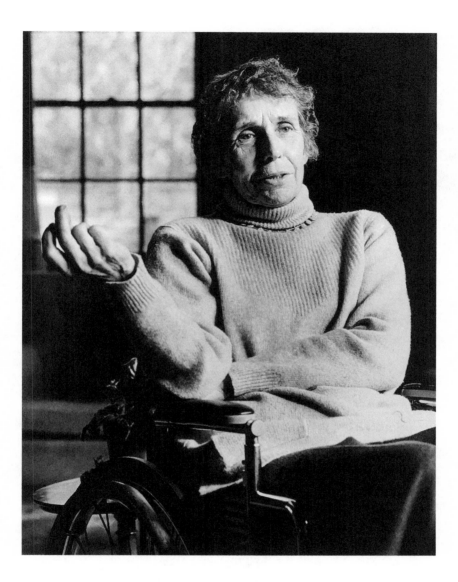

1. Portrait of Nackey Scripps Loeb taken in the early 1980s. Courtesy of Union Leader Corporation. Used with permission.

2. Nackey Scripps Loeb shows off a salmon she caught while fishing in the Canadian wilderness during the summer of 1978. The fishing trip was her first since she was paralyzed in a Jeep accident the year before. Courtesy of Union Leader Corporation. Used with permission.

3. President Richard Nixon shakes hands with Nackey Scripps Loeb at a
White House luncheon while William Loeb looks on in 1971. Nixon was
the first of three presidents Nackey would visit at the White House. Public
domain image on file at the Nackey S. Loeb School of Communications,
Manchester, New Hampshire. Used with permission.

4. Nackey Scripps Loeb meets with President Ronald Reagan in Boston in early 1983. Public domain image on file at the Nackey S. Loeb School of Communications, Manchester, New Hampshire. Used with permission.

Reprint From Manchester Union Leader Thursday Sept. 26, 1957

5. Editorial cartoon opposing government-mandated school integration, drawn by Nackey Scripps Loeb in 1957. The image quickly became popular among segregationists and white supremacists in the South, appearing on pamphlets, posters, and bumper stickers. Courtesy of Union Leader Corporation. Used with permission.

TRUTH IN PACKAGING

6. Editorial cartoon by Nackey Scripps Loeb, undated. Courtesy of Union Leader Corporation. Used with permission.

A Personal Connection 6

During Nackey's first decade as publisher, she faced a host of business challenges. Few of them, though, worried her quite as much as the *Boston Globe*'s plan to open a bureau in Manchester and add a New Hampshire section to its Sunday edition.[1] The prospect of new competition was concerning, but she also loathed the idea of what she viewed as a left-wing paper encroaching on her territory. A few weeks before the *Globe*'s new edition was set to debut in the spring of 1987, Nackey called on an old friend for help. In a letter to President Reagan, she lamented the expansion of a paper that had printed "many nasty anti-Reagan editorials" and requested he grant her newsroom an exclusive interview. "We can think of no better way to greet them than with a story featuring such an interview with you. It would truly be of assistance to us."[2] Reagan obliged, and the story, written from an interview conducted at the White House by Joe McQuaid and star political reporter John DiStaso, appeared on the front page of the *Union Leader* on the same day that the *Globe*'s first New Hampshire edition hit the streets.

Arranging the interview with Reagan was a stunt worthy of old-fashioned newspaper wars. It failed to beat back the *Globe*, but it reminded readers near and far that the *Union Leader* was a unique publication and Nackey was an unusual kind of publisher. She understood that she hadn't just inherited a newspaper; she had inherited its audience—or, rather, its two audiences. One shared geography; the other, ideology. She described them in her very first editorial as publisher when she wrote about serving "the people of New Hampshire and the citizens of this country."[3] Throughout her career she worked to cultivate both groups, amassing influence in ways splashy and subtle. Nackey invested time and money to get the *Union Leader* into people's homes and make it stand out from other sources of information. She believed most newspapers had become too neutral, too aloof, and too detached from people's daily lives. She wanted her readers to feel a personal connection with the *Union Leader* and to view it "as though it were an entity rather than simply a mechanism to bring in the ads or the news."[4]

That job got both easier and harder during her first decade as publisher. Advancements in communication technology provided new platforms to amplify the paper's editorial voice. At the same time, the *Union Leader*'s local audience underwent tremendous change. Between 1980 and 1990, New Hampshire's population grew sharply, surpassing a million as families from the Boston area looked north for cheaper housing. This made the region around Manchester one of the fastest growing areas in the nation, with suburban developments replacing dairy farms and apple orchards.[5] (The state's politics inched leftward during this time, but New Hampshire held on to its main claim to conservatism as the legislature refused to pass broad-based sales or income taxes.) More people meant more demand for news, and the *Globe*—which operated its bureau until the summer of 2001—wasn't the only media outlet that saw the opportunity for growth. A Manchester-based television station, WMUR, had been on the air for decades, but it became a more significant player during the 1980s, when it expanded its news operation to cover the entire state.[6] New Hampshire's eight smaller daily newspapers also attempted to capitalize on the population boom by widening their coverage areas, upgrading their printing presses, and launching Sunday editions. There were also forty weekly papers and three dozen radio stations scattered across the state, many with small but tenacious newsrooms that grew during this time.[7]

To compete, Nackey made significant improvements to the *Union Leader*'s operations. When she became publisher in 1981, her company's financial performance lagged behind the rest of the industry. One reason was the unusually large amount of space the paper devoted to news and opinion. It was also still producing both morning and afternoon editions, a longstanding practice that most newspaper publishers abandoned by the end of the twentieth century. Nackey refused to cut back on content, but eliminating the afternoon edition was her first major managerial decision.[8] She then tackled a slew of production problems that were hindering growth. The prepress systems were obsolete; the phones were unable to handle increased call volume from readers looking to place classified ads; and the mailroom's machine for adding inserts to the papers was so clunky that employees put in overtime stuffing circulars by hand. Distribution was also a constant challenge, with outgoing newspapers and incoming freight sharing a single loading dock.

Nackey's biggest and most expensive headache, though, was her printing operation. The press was downright ancient, and workers had to stop it several times during a typical run to manually load rolls of newsprint. Many of these issues improved in the early 1980s, when the company took over an adjacent building, creating space for three more loading docks and a new mailroom. Nackey also oversaw a number of design changes that gave the paper a more modern look, sometimes sending her managers sketches of new concepts she had developed.[9] The upgrades she made—along with a growing population and a strong economy—helped the *Union Leader* increase its operating margin from 6 percent in 1981 to 20 percent in 1986. Circulation improved, too, outpacing the national average throughout the 1980s.[10] By 1988 the *Union Leader*'s official circulation was 69,875 on weekdays and 89,679 on Sundays. Its closest competitor was the *Globe*, which reported a New Hampshire circulation of 31,363 on weekdays and 62,853 on Sundays.[11]

The newsroom staff grew too. Nackey supported McQuaid's request to hire more reporters; by the mid-1980s the full-time editorial staff hovered around seventy, and the paper had a stable of two dozen freelance regional reporters.[12] (The *Union Leader* wasn't alone in expanding its editorial staff during that time. By most counts, the size of U.S. newspaper newsrooms peaked in 1990.)[13] The focus on local news was intense, recalled Tom Fahey, who spent more than three decades as a reporter at the *Union Leader*, first as a correspondent and eventually as statehouse bureau chief. Every week each correspondent was expected to produce a feature story for the Sunday edition that illustrated some aspect of daily life on their beat. "Fifty-two features a year," Fahey said. "It wasn't easy, but they wanted that stuff. It was a New Hampshire paper, and they wanted all of the New Hampshire stories in there, hard and soft news."[14]

Newspapering was Nackey's family business, and she viewed many of her employees like family. "If someone was in trouble at the paper, she was the person to go to," said Dirk Ruemenapp, who worked as the Sunday editor and later became the company's executive vice president.[15] When Nackey learned about the sudden death of the mother of two paper boys, she ordered one of her managers to send the family a check for $300 to help make ends meet.[16] Another time, she organized a donation drive to help an employee whose adult child had lost everything in a fire. She interacted the most with department heads and other managers, a function of both her schedule and the culture of a company with multiple labor unions. But she tried to get to know rank-and-file workers as much as possible. She was a regular presence at company picnics and softball games and especially enjoyed meeting her employees' children. Each month, staff members celebrating birthdays were invited to join her for cake and chitchat.[17] She also made a point of leaving her office to visit various departments, meet with guests, or grab a sandwich from the vending machine. On one Halloween she caused a ripple of surprised laughter as she toured the office wearing a mask that made her look like Alf, a fictional, wise-cracking puppet who starred in a popular sitcom in the 1980s.[18]

"She was a classy lady," said Tom Thibeault, who worked at the *Union Leader* for nearly three decades, starting in 1977 as an office boy and eventually serving as the chief of photography. "You could pick up the phone and call her house and ask her a question, and she'd talk to you. People who have money tend to be pretentious, but she wasn't that way. She was very, very down to earth." Thibeault got to know Nackey better

A Personal Connection

than most other staffers did because of his various leadership roles with the Manchester Newspaper Guild, the union representing many of the paper's employees. Relations with management were sometimes tense; one round of contract negotiations devolved into a picket line of employees chanting, "Two-four-six-eight, Mrs. Loeb negotiate!" But Thibeault says both Nackey and her husband treated their workers well. "If you go around, you find there are publishers that just pull some real wild things, but I thought she did a good job," he said. "She really cared."[19]

Although Nackey often worked from home, she was deeply involved in daily operations, using memos, phone calls, and weekly staff meetings to guide the *Union Leader*'s long-term strategy. She didn't shy away from making tough business decisions, but she preferred to provide her deputies with options as opposed to direct orders. She read industry journals, circling and underlining key points before sending articles along to various managers. She also sought advice from other publishers, including several members of the Scripps family. She and her older brother Charles, still chairman of the Scripps-Howard board, seemed to have set aside their McCarthy-era political differences enough to maintain a robust correspondence. In between sharing updates on their children and grandchildren, they discussed circulation numbers and newsprint recycling, printing press technology, and employee health care plans. Nackey also consulted with her cousin Jim Scripps, who ran a small chain of newspapers out west. When she sent him a stack of *Union Leaders* to review, he responded that while the content was strong, the print quality was poor. "You are right," Nackey wrote back, lamenting the limitations of her outdated press. "We could do better. Believe me, I continue to harass the editors on a fairly steady basis, especially concerning photo reproduction."[20]

About halfway through the 1980s, Nackey hired a consultant to advise her on how to modernize the *Union Leader* and capitalize on New Hampshire's population boom. John Morton, now retired, remembers his visits to Manchester well because Nackey and her newspaper were so unusual. "Knowing their aggressive conservative approach to things,

I was expecting her to be bristly," he said. "But she was a very nice lady." Most of the papers he worked with were bland, but the *Union Leader* displayed, as he wrote in his report at the time, "an openness to controversy that is rare in most U.S. newspapers."[21] Morton also remembers Nackey's determination to distribute the paper to every corner of the state, something that was neither easy nor cheap given New Hampshire's harsh winters and unpaved roads. "I admired her for that," Morton said. "She really had her community at heart, and she cared more about that than about making more money, which she easily could have done by cutting back their circulation."[22]

Serving the local community was important to Nackey, but she also knew that a bigger audience meant more political influence. Although most of the *Union Leader*'s content was too parochial to appeal to anyone outside the Granite State, its editorials and opinion columns attracted a geographically diverse audience. Throughout her tenure Nackey devised ways to build new connections with the powerful, the like-minded, and the curious around the country. Under William Loeb the *Union Leader* had a small but loyal national audience that got larger with each new presidential primary season. Developments in communication technology, such as the rise of C-SPAN, gave Nackey more tools to reach those readers. Mail subscriptions were a key piece of her strategy, and the circulation department usually received a flurry of new requests every time Nackey appeared on television. Her on-air commentary lacked the volume and rapid-fire cadence endemic to modern political talk shows. Instead, Nackey remained calm, polite, and when pressed on her conservative ideology, unwavering. She didn't love the limelight, but she understood that TV was a useful platform. "If I can sell a lot of papers this way or get a few points across, it's worth the effort," she wrote to a friend.[23]

New Hampshire's first-in-the-nation presidential primary always magnified the attention given to the *Union Leader*. As the 1988 election cycle opened, Nackey wanted to do more to insert her paper's editorial voice into the national conversation. She developed a free monthly newsletter called the *Union Leader Reader* that aggregated the paper's

A Personal Connection

editorials, columns, political cartoons, and other opinion content. It was a hit in terms of messaging if not in terms of financing (McQuaid still regrets not including ads in its design), and it quickly gained a loyal following. A member of the Council of Conservative Citizens thanked Nackey for creating the *Reader*, describing how he made copies of certain editorials to share with "opinion molders" in his community.[24] (The Council of Conservative Citizens started in 1985 as a reboot of the White Citizens' Council.) Journalists at other right-leaning newspapers were also appreciative. Edward Fike, editorial page editor of the *San Diego Union Tribune*, was thrilled whenever a newsletter appeared in his mail. "I remain a faithful reader," he said, "and sometimes reprint your stuff."[25] Another fan was Senator Jesse Helms of North Carolina, a politician Nackey had long admired.[26] "The *Reader*," he wrote her in the spring of 1987, "is a remarkable service for conservatives. You are doing more for 'the cause' than two dozen politicians could ever hope to accomplish."[27]

Nackey's heavy investments in both local news coverage and national outreach illustrate her complex relationship with mainstream journalism. She was a fierce advocate for an independent, watchdog press. Under her leadership the Union Leader Corporation won important court cases related to New Hampshire's right-to-know law, including two that were successfully argued in front of the state supreme court. In one, journalists were granted access to a videotape of a police officer conducting a field sobriety test. In the other, the paper prevailed in its request for documents related to a public-private real estate partnership.[28] Both decisions are still widely cited by those seeking public documents in the Granite State. Nackey also worried about the long-term effects of chain ownership on the quality of local news, a rather prescient concern given how modern megapublishers like GateHouse Media have gutted once-robust local newspapers, including some in New Hampshire.

At the same time, she viewed the national media as biased and part of an orchestrated effort to "weaken the conservative leadership that promises to restore our country."[29] Although she stressed that other news outlets had a First Amendment right to publish what they pleased, she often used her editorials to challenge their coverage. "Much of the liberal news media in America . . . just doesn't like Ronald Reagan or the conservative positions for which he stands," she wrote in early 1983. "It's as if they've decided that now is the time to get Reagan and to hell with any pretense of responsible journalism in the bargain."[30] In stories about apartheid in South Africa, she saw "propaganda . . . played up big by the liberal media . . . part of a well-orchestrated attempt by the Communists and their well-meaning dupes to destroy one more free world ally."[31] During Bill Clinton's reelection campaign, she complained that he was supported by "the liberal media, the TV commentators and columnists and 'interpretive reporters.'"[32]

Nackey disliked the overall tone of television network news, once complaining in a letter to a friend that "they remind me of the old children's story about Chicken Little running around in circles saying 'the sky is falling, the sky is falling.' However, it could turn out a lot more like the fable where the boy kept crying 'wolf!' 'wolf!' and finally people become so bored with all the talk about ozone layers and radon and fallout and acid rain that when a real crisis comes along, we will simply turn away."[33] She sought information outside traditional news sources, subscribing to a variety of conservative newsletters and magazines and, later in life, developing an affinity for talk radio. Nackey was a self-proclaimed "C-SPAN junkie" and often recommended it to friends. Once, she went even further, paying to have a satellite dish installed at Mel and Gale Thomson's farm in honor of their fiftieth wedding anniversary. "No one with your beliefs should be expected to survive if your only source of television news is the Dan Rather/Tom Brokaw, etcetera types," she wrote. "With your satellite dish, you will be able to turn to C-SPAN, which guarantees sanity in this crazy and wonderful country of ours."[34]

Like many conservatives, Nackey was especially irked by coverage of the Iran-Contra affair, a long-simmering and much-politicized scandal that started when members of Reagan's administration secretly sold weapons to Iran and funneled the profits to rebels fighting against

A Personal Connection

Nicaragua's socialist government. "I notice the news media are now calling it a scandal, as if horrendous deeds have already been proved to have been committed," Nackey wrote to a reader in late 1986. "They also have tried to compare it with Watergate. However, the main difference there was that Watergate was the wrong thing to do and it was done for the wrong reason. The handling of the Iran-Contra affair was, I think, the wrong way to do it, but it was done for the right reason, which was to try and hold back the communists from taking over Central America and also from having an opening to the warm waters of the Persian Gulf and the oil supplies there."[35]

During the final years of Reagan's term, she began to worry that Iran-Contra would tarnish his legacy. She encouraged him in frequent letters to "bypass these so-called experts in the media by talking directly to the people. If you do this often, and if you stand firm when you do it, you can make them understand what is at stake in places like Nicaragua."[36] She wrote a number of editorials in support of Reagan's administration. As the investigation and congressional hearings wore on, she also rallied support for Oliver North, a Marine Corps officer who claimed partial responsibility for the arms sale and, to many, became the public face of the scandal. In Nackey's mind he was a hero "who belongs in another time—when duty, honor and country were ideals of ALL young people to follow."[37] During the summer of 1987, Nackey encouraged readers to voice their support for North. "Instead of sitting around beefing, there is a good way to satisfy our frustrations, exert our rights as citizens and be constructive," she wrote. Then she listed addresses for North, his attorney, and his legal assistance fund. She also included names and contact information for members of Congress involved in the Iran-Contra hearings.[38]

During the spring of 1989, Nackey took her support of North even further by inviting him to New Hampshire to give a speech at a Memorial Day event sponsored by the *Union Leader*. She paid North's speaking fee—$25,000—and, before the talk, hosted a private, prime rib dinner for North, his family, and a small group of special guests.[39] The event was announced in the paper, and within several days tickets were sold out. A few protesters gathered outside the downtown Manchester venue, but North received an otherwise warm reception from loyal *Union Leader* readers. He was amazed at how enthusiastically the crowd greeted Nackey. A few days after his talk, he wrote to her, "Only in Manchester, New Hampshire could the publisher of the newspaper receive the overwhelming welcome that you did that night."[40]

A growing audience in New Hampshire and beyond meant that there was no way the old printing press could keep up with production demands. As circulation continued to rise during the late 1980s, Nackey and her managers decided the Union Leader Corporation needed a new production plant. At first Nackey planned to keep the main offices downtown and build a satellite printing warehouse elsewhere, but she eventually chose to move the entire operation to a new complex in an industrial park a few miles away. This strategy was trendy among newspaper owners at the time, although John Morton, the consultant, advised the *Union Leader* (and many of his other clients) against it, arguing it was important to maintain a presence in the center of the community. "They succumbed to what I came to call the empire syndrome," he said. "They really wanted to build a monument. A lot of newspaper owners did. They wanted to build a castle out on the edge of town and move everything there."[41]

Erecting a printing plant is an enormous undertaking. The design and permitting process took more than a year, and as both a businesswoman and a proponent of small government, Nackey grew frustrated with regulatory requirements. The *Union Leader*'s new property stretched across more than twenty acres; the building included more than thirty-five thousand square feet of office space and enough room for a massive printing operation. The press arrived in thirty-three separate deliveries, each one weighing between 3,500 and 5,000 pounds. "That's a heck of a lot machinery not only to pay for, but to put in place," Nackey wrote to a friend.[42]

During construction, the *Union Leader*'s circulation topped one hundred thousand—a significant milestone that belied the economic troubles on the horizon.[43] While workers were assembling the new press and office furniture was arriving by the truckload, the national economy was slowing down. New Hampshire's manufacturing sector was hit especially hard, advertising revenue stagnated, and Nackey grew worried. She made several trips to the construction site, and when she saw all of the beams in place for the first time, she realized just how big the building would be. "If I were not frightened before, I really am now," she wrote in a letter. "But it is a necessary move."[44]

In August 1990 the Union Leader Corporation left its downtown offices. As trucks packed with boxes rumbled away, Tom Thibeault and several other newsroom staffers leaned out a window holding a banner painted with "–30–" (a symbol journalists sometimes use to signal the end of a story).[45] Nackey honored her late husband by naming the road around the new property William Loeb Drive; when the U.S. flag outside was raised for the first time, a group of marines from the local barracks led the ceremony.[46] She was thrilled with the capabilities of the new press and sent copies of the paper to friends, family members, and newspaper publishers around the country. In the fall the company hosted two open houses. The first was for advertisers and special guests; Nackey hired a local actor to entertain them by playing George Washington. The second, for the general public, attracted more than three thousand people, and Nackey greeted many of them herself. "I have never shaken so many hands or signed so many autographs in my life," she wrote, joking that it was a good thing she was left-handed because she could do both at the same time. "But it was a real thrill to see the enthusiasm of the folks who came to visit."[47]

With the new building and new presses came a sweeping redesign of the *Union Leader* and *New Hampshire Sunday News*. Most of the changes were intended to make the papers look more modern, but one update forced Nackey to reconsider the role of the opinion section. The op-ed pages had long been reserved exclusively for conservative columnists.[48] The lack of ideological diversity worried Morton, and he urged Nackey and her editors to add some moderate voices to the mix. Morton admired the *Union Leader*'s strong editorial voice, but he cautioned that "conservatism should not be a straitjacket." The paper had liberal subscribers who, he said, "read the newspaper for the satisfaction of being outraged." But he also suspected the paper was losing out on new readers who didn't identify with any of the opinions it supported. "If the first duty of a newspaper is to be read," Morton wrote, "that duty would be better served by attracting those put off by the uniformly conservative view of the opinion pages."[49]

Nackey and her managers heeded Morton's suggestion and began occasionally highlighting a liberal column or two on the opinion pages. Longtime readers were flabbergasted and accused Nackey of selling the *Union Leader*'s soul. "I try to explain to them that we are just as conservative as we ever were," she wrote in a memo, noting that she hadn't heard anything yet from left-leaning readers. "I suspect the liberals might be in a state of shock. Then again, they might be worried that the weakness of their ideas might be exposed."[50] (The change didn't stop Nackey from promoting conservative voices in her newspaper and beyond. Around the same time, she was publishing occasional columns by Oliver North, who by then was president of the Freedom Alliance, an advocacy group that promotes military service and hawkish foreign policy. Nackey also encouraged him to consider starting a TV show.)[51]

Aside from adding a few liberal columns, Nackey's desire to attract new readers never diluted her political ideology. She knew many people disliked her paper's editorial viewpoint, but she believed dissent was crucial to a functioning democracy. "I don't care if they agree or disagree," she said. "If they can get themselves involved, I think that is what America should be. . . . If we can excite people with our editorials, not with our news stories, we go at it."[52] Nackey sent occasional memos reminding her editors to keep news and opinion separate in local coverage, and even her critics admitted she did a better job than her husband of drawing a line between the two. Still, her personal politics shaped the *Union Leader*'s content in other ways.

In 1984, for instance, she refused to distribute an issue of *Parade* magazine because it contained material she thought promoted sexual promiscuity.[53] (The cover story in question, headlined "Sex in America Today," summarized the results of interviews with 1,100 Americans about their sex lives. Several other newspapers, including the *Chattanooga News-Free Press* in Tennessee, also pulled the magazine.)[54] A few years later, she criticized a *Sunday News* editor for using a wire story that she described as "out-and-out anti–South Africa propaganda." The piece appeared deep in the local section, under the headline "South African Miners, Mostly Blacks, Endure Heat, Danger, Digging for Gold." It documented the grim working conditions at one of the country's gold mines, explaining that because of their race, 90 percent of the miners were "barred by apartheid from advancing any farther in an industry that drives South Africa's economy." The story was written by an Associated Press staffer and was the kind of detail-heavy feature that foreign correspondents often file, but to Nackey it ran counter to the paper's editorial view. "Considering our support of South Africa, in spite of our opposition to apartheid, it is unfortunate that it appeared in our paper. . . . As we use wire services quite often in the *Sunday News*, I think we should be very careful to look them over, because in these days of so-called 'interpretive journalism,' there are many stories where the reporter's bias seeps through."[55]

One of Nackey's most controversial editorial decisions involved a popular comic strip called *For Better or For Worse*, which in 1993 featured a character who came out as gay. Nackey, who sometimes referred to gay people as "sodomites" and "radical perverts" in her editorials, was outraged and refused to publish the strip until the story arc was over.[56] "Creator Lynn Johnston has now decided to join the political propaganda ranks and use her strip to promote homosexuality as a normal, acceptable and morally justified lifestyle," Nackey wrote in an editorial. "We respect her desire to express her opinion. It is perfectly permissible for her to write editorials and articles, so long as she labels them as such. But as to her comic strip, we think it improper for her to camouflage her editorial comments as entertainment, especially when it is in a section widely read by children."[57]

Nackey wasn't the only publisher to pull *For Better or For Worse*, but the group was small. Seven papers canceled the strip outright, and about a dozen others asked for substitute content or temporarily replaced it with another comic. In an interview with the *Boston Globe*, Nackey described her decision by saying, "I don't like hatred, but at the same time I think some things in the world should be hated because of their corrupting influence. I think we should hate those things which are degrading and repulsive and bring down the moral basis on which this country is founded. Acceptance of homosexuality as being correct and morally proper is one of those things."[58]

Her decision drew a mixed reaction from readers in New Hampshire and far beyond. Some applauded her decision. Others were furious. "I'm a gay male who pays taxes and makes decisions in my community just like the next guy," one reader wrote. Someone who signed a letter "Clear-Headed Heterosexual" wrote, "One day in Manchester you will have a teen suicide. It will be determined that the victim was despondent over his or her sexuality. . . . When, not if, this next suicide happens, please give yourself partial credit." A college student canceled his subscription, saying, "Due to your homophobic views, I will start buying another local paper. It is the 1990s, and homophobia has no place in our society—especially the media."[59]

Nackey usually personally responded to every piece of mail she received, but so many people wrote to her about the comic strip that she drafted form letters. To her supporters, she reiterated her belief that the strip had no place in a "family newspaper." To her critics, she wrote, "We all have a right to our opinions, and I am glad that you felt free to express yours."[60]

A Personal Connection

Dear Mrs. Loeb   7

Nackey spent many of her days at home on her farm, working near a picture window that looked out on rolling hills, horse pastures, and a row of birdfeeders busy with swallows, purple finches, and gray squirrels. A painting of a little boy waking up in a Pullman train berth hung on one of the walls, reminding Nackey of the many cross-country trips she made as a child.[1] Each morning, she completed exercises to keep her limbs healthy, had something to eat (Carnation Instant Breakfast was a staple), and watched the news shows, often pausing to jot down notes. Grandkids, farm hands, and the occasional hired caregiver might filter through. A few times a week, managers from the *Union Leader*, and sometimes Nackey's secretary, came by for meetings. But even when Nackey worked in solitude, she was not alone. The *Union Leader* claimed that it published more letters than any other newspaper in the country. What appeared on its pages, though, was miniscule compared to the amount of mail Nackey received. Tending to that vast universe of correspondents consumed much of her time and turned her home office into an under-the-radar hub of national political activism and debate.

It's unclear how the *Union Leader*'s editors compared their letter tallies to other publications, but there was indeed a lot of space devoted to readers' points of view. Most editions of the paper featured multiple pages of letters; the annual total usually surpassed three thousand. Nackey frequently encouraged readers to write even more. "Keep your letters coming, whether friendly or critical," she said in an editorial. "We are glad to have the opportunity to let all of you have your say. This free exchange of ideas is the very essence of democracy and is—or should be—a most important function for a newspaper."[2] The *Union Leader*'s wide-open policy attracted contributors from across the ideological spectrum and around the world. The paper would publish any letter it received, with a few rules: Keep it short (usually less than a few hundred words); don't insult another person's religion; and for submissions from outside New Hampshire, include a mailing label as proof of subscription—something the Loebs started requiring during the 1970s, when out-of-state letters began to overpower Granite State voices.[3]

Most of Nackey's mail was standard fare for a local newspaper: missives from the opinionated, the paranoid, the lonely, and the aggrieved. She also heard from the traditionally powerful—presidential hopefuls, members of New Hampshire's congressional delegation, and assorted government officials. Her most devoted correspondents, though, were right-wing activists scattered across the country. Before the blogosphere and Facebook, before 4chan and Reddit, before viral emails, Twitter, and memes, activists on the far right, the far left, and other ideological fringes communicated through loose networks of newsletters, pamphlets, and zines.[4] These kinds of publications were crucial to the right's resurgence at the end of the twentieth century. As communication scholar James Brian McPherson explains, "Direct mail, which for conservatives became anything but 'junk mail,' did more than any other medium to build the movement."[5] The activists who corresponded with Nackey had different causes, goals, and life experiences, but they all saw her as a crucial node in their burgeoning network. Her *Union Leader* was to them a conservative clearinghouse in an information ecosystem they believed was biased against them.

Parts of Nackey's network dated back to when William Loeb was still alive. He, too, corresponded regularly with people all over the world. During their marriage, one of her chief duties was helping him manage the mail. They often discussed the contents of letters, and in his replies, William Loeb would sometimes summarize Nackey's opinions along with his own.[6] She was also responsible for distributing Christmas cards, a mundane-sounding chore that, because of the couple's

Dear Mrs. Loeb

political position, helped Nackey build significant social capital and a massive Rolodex. Each year, she designed an original card (usually a crisp line drawing of a winter scene or a religious symbol) and had hundreds of copies made. The cards went to friends and family and also to power brokers in the conservative movement. One address list from the 1970s, for instance, includes the entire board of the National Rifle Association—a previously apolitical organization that was at the time becoming closely aligned with the New Right.[7]

After she became publisher, Nackey attracted new far-flung followers who saw her on TV, picked up the *Union Leader Reader*, or read copies of her editorials passed on by like-minded friends. The profile of Nackey that Mel Thomson wrote for *Conservative Digest* in early 1987 also yielded a flurry of mail from new fans.[8] The Loebs' bicoastal lifestyle and Nackey's family ties to the West further extended her geographic reach, with mail often arriving from Nevada and Southern California. Some people wrote Nackey just a handful of times or surfaced whenever a primary approached, but correspondence with her most loyal contacts lasted for years. Their collective musings are a barometer of the mood of the conservative rank and file throughout the final two decades of the twentieth century. During the 1980s the Soviet Union played the role of chief boogeyman. Later it was the threat of free trade and the so-called New World Order. They decried U.S. sanctions on South Africa, complained about restrictive gun laws, lamented the loss of local control, and generally believed the Republican Party was abandoning both traditional values and its conservative base.

Their mail came in many forms: neatly typed letters on corporate stationary, handwritten postcards, nearly illegible screeds stuffed in envelopes thick with clippings. Nackey sent her responses—and she almost always responded to the mail she received—in long white envelopes with the initials NSL stamped in bold black type over the *Union Leader*'s return address. Her replies were polite and chatty, addressing the topic at hand but also usually including a few sentences about the weather, the antics of various farm animals, or the latest accomplishments of her three beloved grandchildren. Nackey and her correspondents trafficked not just in ideas but in gifts. They sent her fresh pecans, jars of sourwood honey, Vidalia onions, and recipe suggestions for the salmon she caught on her summer fishing trips. In return, Nackey would ship them bottles of maple syrup from Mel Thomson's farm and, to especially loyal writers, bags of his homemade pancake mix. They shared personal anecdotes, too, commiserating about health problems and celebrating family milestones.

One of Nackey's most enduring correspondents was Clayton Brown, a former member of the Georgia legislature who ran a furniture store in Griffin, a small city south of Atlanta. The Loebs first got to know Brown when he was an enthusiastic member of Jimmy Carter's "peanut brigade" during the 1976 primary. They never met him in person, but he exchanged regular letters with William Loeb and later with Nackey.[9] By the early 1980s, Brown had migrated to the GOP. In his letters he gave the perspective of a Republican everyman, worried about how government policies would affect his business, his family, and his community. When New Hampshire was considering legislation that would allow interstate banking, Brown wrote at length about Georgia's experiences with a similar change, arguing that consolidation would make it difficult for small banks and small businesses like his to thrive. "Once the biggies are in full control, they will call the shots and this will not be healthy for the public," he wrote to Nackey in the spring of 1987. "I think we are in a helluva mess."[10]

Nackey also heard from the more extreme corners of the political right. During her first years as publisher, she received frequent press releases—and, just before Christmas 1982, a hand-embroidered handkerchief—from Anne Neamon, the national coordinator of Citizens For God and Country, a Virginia-based group that lobbied for "general Christian founding principles."[11] Neamon was well known in Northern Virginia for her opposition to sex education and her support of school prayer. In 1984 she attracted the attention of the *Washington Post* when she convinced the National Park Service to include a nativity scene in its holiday display near the White House. The origin and size of Neamon's organization were rather opaque. She once said publicly that she was the group's only member, but later she denied it, telling the *Post* that she "could not reveal the group's address, her home address or her age for fear of retaliation by Communists."[12] Her rambling, hard-to-decipher submissions to the *Union Leader* accused the Library of Congress of giving biased information to public schools about classroom prayer, advocated for a return to "Christian ethics in government," and called Martin Luther King Jr. a "subversive" who didn't deserve a holiday in his honor.[13] Her correspondence with Nackey appears to have been short-lived, however. The *Union Leader* published several of Neamon's letters but eventually curtailed her writing when it routinely exceeded the paper's limits on letter length.[14]

A longer-lasting, if similarly extreme, contributor was Alyn Denham, a Tennessee man who in 1980 started a newsletter called *Americans for Sane Policies*. He claimed to travel widely and to have confidential sources deep within the U.S. intelligence apparatus; his mission was to report "information the media and the U.S. government will not tell you."[15] Each edition of his newsletter was packed with capital letters, aggressive underlining, and the kind of over-the-top rhetoric that would look just right on an early blog. An issue from 1987, for instance, opened with the slogan "It is useless for the sheep to pass resolutions in favor of vegetarianism while the wolf remains of a different opinion." The lead story claimed that senior citizens would be required to pay for treatment for people with AIDS. Other articles called *The New Republic* a "Red rag" and described a variety of vague but dangerous secret plots by the U.S. government.

Denham encouraged readers to quote his publication in letters to their local newspapers or to cite his work when calling in to radio talk shows. He also sometimes excerpted Nackey's writing. "Your editorials are like a breath of spring after the blizzards of a liberal winter," he once wrote to her.[16] Nackey thought of him as "a strange soldier of fortune type, a very patriotic gentleman who is willing to speak his mind in his publication."[17] In addition to printing some of his letters in the *Union Leader*, she sent him money, about fifty dollars a year, to help defray the cost of producing and mailing his newsletter. "It is good to know there are people like you who are willing to spread the word," she once wrote. "If I can help I certainly will."[18]

Another of Nackey's fringe correspondents called himself Michael Barrow. His legal name was Michael Bobrow (why he used a pseudonym is unclear), and he was the county committeeman for the Conservative Party of New York State. In the mid-1980s he ran for the Bronx city council on the Conservative ticket. During that campaign the *New York Daily News* described him as "an activist in the clergy-conservative coalition against gay rights."[19] He was a bit of a gadfly, too, writing more letters than Nackey could respond to and sometimes tying up *Union Leader* secretaries for hours with long, rambling phone calls.[20] He and Nackey corresponded mostly about efforts by gay rights groups to participate in community celebrations or hold Pride events. In one of her letters, Nackey pondered Bobrow's ongoing attempts to stop these kinds of gatherings. "No one quite knows how to handle the situation without seeming to be bigoted," she wrote. "However, there is nothing wrong with being bigoted if you are being bigoted for the right reason."[21]

She exchanged letters with traditional political activists too. One was Mark Bablin, a New Jersey man who devoted much of his time to campaign work. He started his political career as a member of the Conservative Party and in the mid-1970s served as a regional coordinator for George Wallace, a pro-segregation Democrat who ran unsuccessfully for president several times.[22] By the time Nackey became publisher, Bablin was aligned with New Jersey's Republican Party. He worked on behalf of GOP candidates, including George H. W. Bush, although he worried about the vice president's ability to project a strong image. "He must be *tougher* on foreign policy," he wrote. "Bush must hammer away at the Democrats' weakness . . . to compensate for his own shortcomings."[23]

Nackey's network was eclectic, and its power manifested in different ways. Sometimes she would connect like-minded letter writers to each other, strengthening activists' relationships across geography. The inverse was true, too, with longtime contributors urging their

Dear Mrs. Loeb

contacts to write to and subscribe to the *Union Leader*.[24] Nackey's editorials were important ideological currency among her followers, and she often sent multiple copies to people she thought were likely to pass them along.[25] Many correspondents also made additional copies to distribute by mail or fax. Once, Denham was so impressed with an editorial Nackey wrote, in which she criticized what she saw as lax U.S. policy toward the USSR, that he reprinted the entire thing, complete with her photo and signature. He also included her mailing address, in case any of his readers wanted to contact her directly.[26]

The network also served as a conduit to the powerful. As publisher of the *Union Leader*, Nackey was in regular contact with members of New Hampshire's congressional delegation and other elected officials. Sometimes she'd pass along material from her correspondents. One example of this involved efforts to find Vietnam War–era prisoners of war rumored to be alive in Southeast Asia. In 1986 Denham traveled to Laos as part of a civilian group that claimed to have found evidence of American POWs still held in captivity. When he returned home, he wrote to Nackey for advice on how to draw attention to the situation. She was unconvinced by the photos Denham sent her as evidence, but she sympathized with his concern and connected him to Representative Bob Smith, a Republican who had long been among the *Union Leader*'s favorite local conservatives. Smith had also traveled to Southeast Asia that year to investigate possible POWs, and at Nackey's urging, Denham wrote him a long letter that she passed along to the congressman. "If you would like to contact him through me rather than directly, let me know," she wrote to Smith. "I will be glad to be the go-between."[27] (Congressional investigations into the fate of POWs continued for years. In a 1993 report, the investigating committee, of which Smith was a member, determined that "there is no proof that U.S. POWs survived, but neither is there proof that one or more did not.")[28]

Another instance in which Nackey transmitted information from her correspondents to people in power occurred during the planning of Pride Week events in New York during the summer of 1989. To mark the celebration and commemorate the twentieth anniversary of the

Stonewall riots, the U.S. Postal Service issued a special stamp cancellation that included the words "lesbian and gay pride." Members and allies of the LGBTQ community were thrilled, pointing to the stamp as the first-ever recognition of Pride Day by a federal agency.[29] Social conservatives, including Nackey and many members of her network, were outraged. It was Bobrow who told her about plans for the stamp; almost immediately, she complained to Senator Gordon Humphrey, a New Hampshire Republican. The senator, in turn, wrote a letter to the postmaster general in which he accused the U.S. Postal Service of violating moral decency standards, and he supplied a copy to Nackey. "To issue such a cancellation is to countenance an activity which is unnatural, unhealthful and objectional to the vast majority of Americans," he wrote. "It constitutes a 'stamp of approval' for homosexuality, which is absolutely the wrong message to come from an agency of government."[30] Nackey also editorialized against the stamp, saying the officials who had approved it "should be taken on a one-way trip to the woodshed."[31]

Nackey's correspondents percolated into her writing in other ways, too. She quoted Brown on several occasions, such as when she reprinted portions of a letter he wrote about the ills of big banks to bolster her argument against interstate banking.[32] In 1989 Nackey used another one of Brown's letters to emphasize her opposition to a state sales tax. In Georgia, Brown wrote, a sales tax increase had done little to reduce the need for other types of taxes, and he worried about the state's financial future. "A broad-based plan will just eventually gut the people and give no relief to the property owner."[33] Nackey also quoted Denham and his newsletter several times. In 1984 she suggested readers look for his op-ed column in that day's paper, calling it "a very good but very discouraging summary of where the United State finds itself after 20 years of appeasing the Soviet Union."[34] Two years later she included in her Labor Day editorial a letter he wrote accusing labor unions of sympathizing with communists. Another time, she quoted an article from Denham's newsletter in an editorial accusing Congress and the press of liberal bias when investigating political scandals.[35]

One of the most profound examples of the network's influence on the *Union Leader*'s editorial stance is a series of events that unfolded shortly before the 1988 primary. Bobrow, the antigay gadfly from New York, was fascinated by the quixotic presidential bid of Democrat William A. Marra, a socially conservative philosophy professor from New Jersey whose campaign literature described him as a "pro-life Democrat" and a "family man against special privileges for homosexuals."[36] In a characteristically long and rambling letter, Bobrow convinced Nackey to do something unusual for the *Union Leader* at the time: issue an endorsement in the Democratic race. Marra had never held elected office, but Bobrow believed he had a shot in the New Hampshire primary. "He's a great guy," he wrote. "Intelligent and a *delight* to listen to."[37] Nackey and Marra talked on the phone at least once—he called to ask her advice on organizing a press conference—and about a week before the primary, she threw her newspaper's support behind his campaign.[38] She encouraged "good conservative New Hampshire Democrats" to consider Marra. "Around the country, people look to our primary to tell them how the voters feel," she wrote. "We have a chance to tell them that there are many here who don't like the pro-abortion, big-spending, anti-nuke, pro-homosexual compromising platform they are being offered on the Democratic side."[39]

Come primary day, Marra won 142 votes, placing eleventh in a twenty-four-person Democratic field. A month later, as Marra's short-lived primary campaign was flickering out, Bobrow wrote Nackey to apologize for pushing him as a candidate.[40] "The Marra fiasco in the New Hampshire Primary must have been a far greater embarrassment to you, putting your prestige and that of the *Union Leader* on the line," he wrote. "I deeply . . . regret my role in causing this embarrassment, though, in fairness to myself, I must stress that I did not foresee that Marra would do *that* horribly."[41] It took Nackey another month to clear out a backlog of mail that had accumulated during the primary. When she finally responded to Bobrow, she didn't mention his apology . . . or Marra.

In general, Nackey shared substantial parts of her correspondents' worldviews, but it's hard sometimes to gauge her opinion on specific issues because she was always so cordial in her responses. Sometimes she would reveal her true feelings when she passed letters along to her editors. Once, she complained to McQuaid about some mail she'd received from members of the John Birch Society, the ultraconservative advocacy group founded in the late 1950s. "These people who want total purity and refuse to face reality certainly do more harm to Reagan than Reagan's enemies do," she wrote.[42] She also sometimes refused to publish letters she received, even those that came from loyal correspondents.

One submission that didn't pass muster came from Denham. In 1990 he sent Nackey a long, disjointed essay that made wide-ranging accusations about a cover-up perpetrated by U.S. elected officials and intelligence agencies in an attempt to "undermine every effort . . . to render aid to every pro-Western resistance movement." Nackey responded with her usual politeness, explaining that the paper had to be "very careful" about verifying the material it published. "You raised some darn good questions and I am going to share this with the editors and also keep it on hand for reference," she wrote, tucking some money into the envelope. "I hope things are going well with you as we all continue the battle. By the way, here's a little something to take care of the postage stamps."[43]

As the 1988 election cycle opened, discontent rippled through Nackey's network. Reagan was about to leave office, and most conservatives were disappointed in the emerging GOP field. "Unfortunately, there still seems to be no candidate on the Republican right with a clear national consensus like Ronald Reagan had in 1980," Bablin wrote. "It almost makes one nostalgic for that era."[44] Brown, meanwhile, was excited that the Democrats had picked Atlanta for the party's summer convention because it would be good for Georgia's image, but he found little else positive about the 1988 elections. The Republican field was "lousy," he wrote. Bush, he worried, would be a weak nominee.[45] Denham was

Dear Mrs. Loeb

busy planning a trip to Nicaragua and didn't have much to say about the primary. Nackey still kept him updated, writing in April of 1987 that "more would-be presidents continue to arrive in New Hampshire. Our editor-in-chief, Joe McQuaid, [says] that the reason this is called the '88 primary is that there are going to be eighty-eight candidates running for president. At least it will be lively, but so far it doesn't look very hopeful."[46]

Nackey feared that without a strong right-wing contender in the primary, the GOP would pick Bush as its nominee, signaling, in her mind at least, the end of her brand of conservatism. More letters poured in from increasingly disenfranchised activists, and Nackey began trying to seed the GOP field with better options. She'd seen this technique work before. Efforts to convince reluctant candidates to run for office are commonly called "draft movements." They've been part of the culture of the New Hampshire primary since Nackey and William Loeb first arrived in the state. The most storied political draft targeted Dwight D. Eisenhower in the 1952 primary. Ike was willing to run but didn't want to campaign, so his supporters threw parties and hosted vaudeville shows to attract crowds in his absence. Their unorthodox techniques worked. Eisenhower won the primary and the White House, although not the *Union Leader*'s endorsement. (The Loebs backed Taft that year.) During the following decade, another draft movement helped push Barry Goldwater into the race and on to the top of the Republican Party's 1964 ticket. (He *did* have the Loebs' support but didn't win New Hampshire, coming in second to Henry Cabot Lodge.) Nackey knew draft movements could fail, too. In 1979, for instance, a group of New Hampshire Democrats recruited Senator Ted Kennedy from Massachusetts to run against incumbent Jimmy Carter in the 1980 primary. Kennedy lost to Carter by ten points and soon ended his campaign.[47]

Still, Nackey was willing to try to bolster the conservative movement's chances in the 1988 election by starting a draft effort of her own. She looked first to her old friend Pat Buchanan, who was finishing a stint as communications director for Reagan's White House. He'd made a few visits to New Hampshire, and she had cheered him on in a couple of front-page editorials. She backed off, though, when he told her privately that he'd decided not to launch a campaign that year.

Instead, Nackey turned to Jeane Kirkpatrick, a political scientist from Oklahoma with a cult following among conservatives. Kirkpatrick was a professor at Georgetown University before Reagan installed her on his National Security Council and named her the first female U.S. ambassador to the United Nations. Although she had no prior experience as a diplomat, Kirkpatrick won Reagan's admiration for what the *New York Times* described as her "strong diplomatic stands and her undiplomatic language."[48] By the late 1980s she'd left the White House and was back at Georgetown. (She'd also officially joined the Republican Party after many years as a rather unorthodox Democrat.) Her connection to Reagan helped her win Nackey's admiration. So did her efforts to advance what became known as the Kirkpatrick doctrine, a philosophy that argued the United States should support dictatorships if those dictatorships stopped the advance of communism. Nackey also suspected Kirkpatrick would excel at the kind of retail politics one needed to win in New Hampshire. During the fall of 1987, she began dropping the former ambassador's name into her editorials. "Here is a lady, but not a feminist," she wrote that September, "one who has tremendous popularity and yet has never had to solicit votes, someone who would make Mr. Gorbachev sit up and take notice."[49] A few weeks later, she called her "a lady with principle who is a firm, frank supporter of the United States of America."[50]

Nackey also gauged the mood of her network of letter writers, many of whom were intrigued by the idea of a Kirkpatrick candidacy. Brown, however, was unsure. "She would make a helluva fine president," he wrote. "But unhappily, she has no charisma or personality appealing to the masses."[51] Other Kirkpatrick critics worried that she wouldn't be accepted by Republican elites because of her former ties to the Democratic Party. Nackey was undeterred, however, and began coordinating her efforts with other prominent conservatives. Locally, Mel Thomson backed the nascent draft movement. Across the country, meanwhile, Kirkpatrick received support from the *San Diego Union*

Tribune in the form of a column written by Edward Fike, the editorial page editor and one of Nackey's longtime friends. "Kirkpatrick," he argued, "would provide the 1988 race conservative horsepower, and she would inspire armies of zealous precinct workers."[52] Nackey also stirred up enthusiasm in Kirkpatrick's home state of Oklahoma by contacting political power brokers there, including Edward Gaylord, the founder of a large media company that included the *Oklahoman*.[53]

About a year before the 1988 New Hampshire primary, Nackey began writing to Kirkpatrick herself, sending copies of key editorials and describing a potential base of support in the Granite State and beyond. "Anytime your name is brought up, people's eyes light up," Nackey wrote in a letter.[54] A Kirkpatrick candidacy had been a fantasy among certain segments of the Republican Party for several years, so there was some swag in circulation, and in another letter, Nackey described a "Kirkpatrick for President" button she had acquired. "I think I will wear it to the office tomorrow," she wrote, "just to see what the reaction is."[55]

Kirkpatrick was surprised to hear from Nackey and to learn that so many people wanted her to run for president. In a series of letters, she explained that she might consider a campaign if, come fall, no other conservative candidates were doing well. The two women continued to correspond, and their letters became longer and friendlier. Nackey provided regular updates on the mood of New Hampshire's electorate and the machinations of the other campaigns. Kirkpatrick was intrigued but had reservations. "I realize in the face of the idea that I am a more traditional woman than I usually think I am—at least more influenced by residual sex-role inhibitions."[56] Nackey persisted, stressing that the 1988 race was "one of the most important elections this country has faced." It was possible, she said, to mount an ambitious campaign without abandoning traditional womanhood. "There is nothing wrong with that and nothing wrong with continuing to be a lady," she wrote. "However, don't underestimate your popularity across this country."[57]

Kirkpatrick remained wary of running, but in the fall of 1987 she agreed to visit New Hampshire for a couple of days. Her itinerary included a speech at a Republican fundraiser, plus a second, more intimate talk at a dinner Nackey helped organize. There, Kirkpatrick spoke to thirty uncommitted Republican activists assembled at a Manchester restaurant for prime rib, baked potatoes, and apple crisp à la mode.[58] The guests were impressed with her speech. So was Nackey, who described the evening in detail to her contacts around the country. "She was overwhelmed by the votes of confidence that she is receiving," Nackey wrote to Fike, "not only from us here at the paper, but from others as well."[59] Kirkpatrick spent the next few weeks considering her options. Nackey waited and hoped. And waited some more. Eventually Kirkpatrick decided not to run, telling Nackey in a letter that she didn't want to subject herself to the intense scrutiny of a campaign.[60] Nackey was disappointed but gracious in her reply. "It isn't a pleasant process," she wrote. "But I suppose in our type of government, it's the way that it gets done and, unfortunately, there are powerful interests that seem to have taken over."[61]

In the weeks that followed, Nackey thought about throwing the *Union Leader*'s support behind a write-in campaign for Kirkpatrick. She decided not to, fearing it would fracture conservatives and help Bush win.[62]

The "Wimp" in Washington   **8**

Without Kirkpatrick, Nackey was unsure who the *Union Leader* should endorse in the 1988 Republican primary. Her dismay with the declared candidates was apparent to anyone who read her newspaper, as was the significance she put on that year's election. Like many on the right, she saw it as a choice between two starkly different versions of government, one exemplified by conservatives like Reagan and the other by Democrats and moderate Republicans. "On one side, Ronald Reagan is the first true representative of the cause to be elected to the White House in modern times," she wrote in an editorial. "On the other side, we have the liberals who insist they know what is best for the people and whose presidents have built governments that attempt to care for every need at home and appease all Communists abroad. . . . How we vote (in the primary) will decide America's future."[1]

Bush remained the establishment favorite but faced multiple challengers, including Senator Bob Dole, televangelist Pat Robertson, Representative Jack Kemp, and former Delaware governor Pierre "Pete" DuPont. Kemp was angling for the right-wing vote, and Nackey tried to like him. His conservative bona fides were, in her mind, top notch. She'd also enjoyed the keynote speech he gave at a dinner that the Zionist Organization of America had held in her honor in 1984. (Nackey was given the Louis D. Brandeis Award that year in recognition of her support for Israel.)[2] Soon, though, her opinion of Kemp soured. His stump speech, she lamented in a letter to Buchanan, went over "like a lead balloon."[3] When Nackey and Kemp met again early in the primary, there was zero chemistry between the two. "He just irritated the hell out of her," one national reporter later recalled. "He never let her get a word in edgewise, and he never convinced her he'd listen to her, much less act the way she wanted."[4]

Dole, meanwhile, was too fond of taxes for Nackey's taste. "If you want a president who will cost you money . . . vote for Bob Dole," she wrote in an editorial a few weeks before the primary.[5] She liked Robertson but worried the country wasn't ready for an evangelical pastor as president. "Nor do we believe that Pat Robertson is ready for the country," she wrote, advising him to stop "smiling at the same time he's talking about serious problems."[6] Instead, the *Union Leader* backed DuPont, a candidate Nackey thought had "more brains and more sense than all the others."[7] The choice surprised the national media and said more about Nackey's dissatisfaction with the other candidates than about DuPont's chances at victory. He had plenty of experience, serving in Congress for six years before becoming Delaware's governor, a post he held from 1977 to 1985; and he espoused conservative policies such as work requirements for welfare recipients, an end to farm subsidies, and government grants for private school tuition.[8] But he wasn't connecting with voters. After a poor showing in Iowa, his campaign rolled into New Hampshire on fumes.

Even Nackey didn't think her endorsement would do much good, but she saw him as the only real option for conservatives. The *Union Leader's* support of DuPont was never about DuPont. Instead, it reflected Nackey's fears that the Republican Party was leaving the Reagan era as a watered-down version of conservatism, one that was too global, too moderate, and too weak. After the votes were counted on primary day, DuPont finished fourth with 10 percent of the vote and soon ended his campaign. Bush, meanwhile, used New Hampshire to resuscitate his campaign after a disappointing third-place finish in Iowa. He won the Granite State with 38 percent, nearly ten points ahead of runner-up Dole. On the Democratic side, former Massachusetts governor Michael Dukakis trounced the competition, with Representative Dick Gephardt coming in a distant second.[9] For weeks after the primary, Nackey continued to lament the state of the race,

The "Wimp" in Washington

blaming the press, the party elites, and the candidates themselves for lackluster options. "What we are being given through the campaign speeches and hollow promises is pure propaganda," she wrote in an editorial in late April. "This is being done with the aid of the liberal news media, which promote their champions and ignore any others. The American people are being sold a bill of goods with no concern for the quality of the merchandise. Given the present choices, we are in for a tough four years ahead."[10]

By early summer it was clear that Bush would be the Republican nominee and Dukakis would be his opponent. There are few things worse in New Hampshire politics than being labeled a Massachusetts liberal, so it's no surprise that Nackey was horrified by the prospect of a Dukakis presidency. She was determined to stop him at all costs, even if it meant supporting Bush in the general election. The endorsement came in June, two months before the Republican National Convention and nearly three years after Nackey and the vice president had dined side by side at the Project '88 tribute to William Loeb. "We remember the good old days—the days when this newspaper said that in no way would it support George Bush," Nackey wrote. "However, now is the time for eating our words, for the alternative could prove disastrous for our country."[11] Instead of championing Bush's credentials, Nackey offered advice. "This is no time for Bush to stick to the safe and easy issues, such as education and drugs and civil rights. Bush can and will lose if he campaigns on the theme of, 'anything they can promise, I can promise better.' The one promise that Bush must make and mean is that he'll return the White House to the philosophy of the first-term Ronald Reagan."[12]

Her public support of Bush remained tepid, but Nackey went on the attack against Dukakis. When he proposed federally subsidized child care, she called it communism. "The Dukakis plan simply bribes the family to turn the children over to the state, a practice more in keeping with Soviet solutions than American."[13] When Dukakis supported legal access to abortion, she said allowing women to choose was against God's will. "The laws of God and morality should not be disobeyed for the sake of convenience."[14] Whenever he talked about his tax plan, she accused him of trying to "make the wealthy into the enemy."[15]

The race between Bush and Dukakis was tight and nasty—a dynamic that Nackey welcomed. "The voters are far from enthusiastic about either candidate," she wrote. "In that case, whoever wants the presidency is going to have to make his opponent even less palatable. Both candidates figure that is a lot easier than changing the minds of lukewarm voters about their own appeal. We say let them at each other."[16] To help Bush, she even offered to do a bit of dirty work on behalf of his campaign by publishing unflattering pictures of Dukakis's wife.

A couple of months before the general election, rumors began to circulate that Kitty Dukakis had burned an American flag at an anti-war protest in the 1960s. The rumor likely originated from Senator Steve Symms, a Republican from Idaho who told his local radio station that photos of Kitty Dukakis and the smoldering flag would "surface before the elections are over." The Dukakis campaign denied the rumors. Kitty Dukakis said that although she had opposed the Vietnam War, she didn't recall ever attending an anti-war protest, much less one where she lit a flag on fire. The Democrats were outraged by the charges and accused the GOP of trying to deflect attention from questions surrounding Republican vice-presidential candidate Dan Quayle's military service during Vietnam. Within a couple of days, Symms backed away from his comments, telling a different radio show that he had no evidence for his claims and he believed Mrs. Dukakis's denials. "I'm happy to know Mrs. Dukakis has never burned an American flag," he said, stressing that he had never seen the photos in question. "I think I'll drop the subject."[17]

Nackey, however, continued to believe that a photo existed. She also suspected the Bush campaign had a copy. In mid-September she sent a letter directly to Bush, offering to publish the picture on the front page of her newspaper. "I know where it could get a proper airing," she wrote. "Obviously, this is something that you, as a candidate, should not touch, but as you know, the *Union Leader* has never been shy about things that appear on its pages!"[18] The photo never surfaced, and neither Bush nor his campaign replied to Nackey's letter.

Bush won the election with 53 percent of the popular vote nationally and 62 percent in New Hampshire. Nackey sent him a note of congratulations, telling him he'd "buried the wimp" during his campaign.[19] Privately, though, she was already thinking in terms of four, not eight, years. She and her network of correspondents declared a quiet defeat for their brand of conservatism and started looking ahead to 1992. They watched Bush's inauguration with resignation, and as the first years of his presidency unfolded, they grew more and more frustrated. The new president, she wrote to Denham in the spring of 1989, is "a compromiser and, unfortunately, he is still a wimp. . . . I am however sensing that across the country there is a general feeling of revolt against those in government who are misusing their power to their own ends."[20] To Bablin, the Republican activist from New Jersey, she lamented that Bush had "won the election but lost the presidency." "Our only hope," she continued, "is that we weather the next two years and then find somebody who can really assume leadership of our nation."[21]

Winter rain fell hard as Nackey's commuter jet took off from the Manchester airport early one morning in January 1990. It was an imperfect time to leave New Hampshire, even for a short trip. The *Union Leader*'s new office complex was taking shape, and the project was consuming huge amounts of her time. "I must have been sitting around twiddling my thumbs before we decided to construct a building," she wrote to friend.[22] The night before, the paper had sponsored an awards dinner that kept her up past midnight, so she was already exhausted. But she still enjoyed peering out the airplane window at the snow-covered hills below. She could see her horse farm on the outskirts of the city, and she marveled at how the fences, house, and barn looked like a pen and ink drawing. Her destination was Washington DC, where the Bush White House was hosting a luncheon for newspaper publishers. To Nackey's surprise, she was on the guest list. Although she'd issued perfunctory congratulations when Bush was inaugurated, Nackey had since produced a steady stream of editorials critical of the new president. Yes, she'd complained about some of Reagan's policies, too, but her problems with Bush were different. During Reagan's tenure, she found fault with individual decisions made by his administration. With Bush she took issue with the ideology of the man himself.

She declared Bush's first one hundred days in office a failure and devoid of any accomplishments. "George Bush ran as a born-again Reagan," she wrote. "But now that he's in office, he seems to be trying to find himself, and we still don't know what that self is. We may very well have a president more interested in being a nice guy than in being a leader."[23] Later, she lamented his foreign policy, saying it was designed to make him look good rather than improve the standing of the United States.[24] In another column, she proclaimed, "Like a woman, hell hath no fury like a conservative scorned, and many conservatives are disappointed with Bush's failure to fulfill his promise of carrying on the Reagan agenda."[25] Nackey saw Bush's list of sins as long and growing: He refused to pardon Oliver North and others involved in Iran-Contra; he was too willing to overlook human rights violations to expand trade with China; his no-new-taxes pledge might not last. She wanted him to be more decisive and more like Reagan, who "started his administration with a simple yet direct base of beliefs: less government, fewer taxes, a strong nation and a proud one."[26]

Still, an invitation from a sitting president—even one with whom she often disagreed—was worth the time and effort of a trip to Washington DC. "I figured if George Bush was broad-minded enough to invite me," Nackey wrote to a friend, "the least I could do was be broad-minded enough to show up."[27] It would be a long and challenging day. On the ground at Dulles Airport, the elevator in the terminal was broken, so she had to perch her wheelchair precariously on the escalator, something she later told multiple people she would never do again. Bush's chief of staff, former New Hampshire governor John Sununu, sent a limo to meet Nackey at the airport. A kind gesture, she thought, but the car didn't have enough space for her chair, so it got

The "Wimp" in Washington

wet hanging out of the trunk while they drove into the city. When they arrived at the White House, the guard station was empty, and they had to wait to get in. These were all minor annoyances that Nackey laughed about later, but she also saw them as examples of government dysfunction. "Washington is certainly a strange and fascinating place with glorious statues representing almost everything and, yet, nothing seems to work," she wrote to one of her brothers. "The funniest thing about it is that nobody seems to mind about all the inconvenience."[28]

The trip wasn't all bad. She had a chance to visit with Oliver North at the Freedom Alliance. He was excited to see Nackey and left his office building to chat with her in the back of the spacious limo so she wouldn't have to transfer in and out of her wheelchair in the rain. At the White House, the décor was gorgeous; the food was good too—"two different wines, fancy soup, beef and all the trimmings, and the kind of dessert that dieters have nightmares about," she later wrote.[29] Over coffee Bush talked about his antidrug program and a few other policy items. When it came time for questions, most of the newspaper publishers in attendance wanted to know about the deficit or foreign policy. Nackey had something different on her mind. Would the president consider pardoning North or John Poindexter, a navy officer implicated in the Iran-Contra scandal? "Really, Nackey," she remembered Bush replying, "that is in the hands of the courts, and it would be inappropriate for me to comment." Although she was dissatisfied with the answer, she was pleased to have brought up the subject.[30]

This trip to Washington DC felt different from the ones she'd made before. During Reagan's first term, she'd been among the honored guests at a picnic to celebrate Women's Equality Day. To her, the event embodied America, as she described in a column that appeared a few days later on the *Union Leader*'s front page. "There is something heart-stopping about the combination of this, the greatest country in the world, and mustard and hot dogs; the combination of small talk and big ideals. . . . [It] makes one realize that just as this is our backyard picnic, this is our government."[31] Her visit to the Bush White House yielded no such accolades; she found the capital gloomy for reasons that had little to do with the rain. The day was a metaphor for the melancholy that had descended upon many corners of the conservative movement in the months after Bush's inauguration. Nackey began contemplating how she and her newspaper might force change in the GOP. By this point in her career, Nackey was both an insider and an outsider. She owned a small but powerful media company in a state that was crucial to national politics. She'd spent nearly a decade as publisher overcoming stereotypes about her gender and disability, amassing a loyal following, and learning to coexist with and sometimes capitalize upon her late husband's enduring legacy. Her network included establishment Republicans, but she was also well connected with and admired by the populist, right-wing fringe. She knew those people were frustrated and, if given the right champion, would be ready to rebel.

In some ways she wanted to see Bush succeed. It would be less messy for the party and less likely to create an opening for the Democrats in 1992. But her worries, both ideological and practical, were mounting. She may have been a conservative activist, but she was also a businesswoman, one whose company was building a multimillion-dollar headquarters at the same time as the economy was slowing down. Ad revenue was flat, and they'd had to reduce the space allotted for news to keep expenses in check.[32] New Hampshire's business climate was terrible, and layoffs were becoming more common, especially at the state's many factories and paper mills. The folder she kept for people inquiring about jobs at the *Union Leader* was growing thicker, and the tone of their cover letters was becoming more desperate. Members of her correspondent network were suffering too. Brown's furniture business was in trouble. Big ticket items, he wrote, were just not in demand, but the local K-Mart and Wal-Mart seemed to be doing just fine.[33] Other connections were irked by Bush's policies and a perceived lack of leadership. When Republican candidates fared poorly in municipal elections in New York and New Jersey in 1989, Bablin blamed apathy among grassroots activists who were adrift without a clear agenda for the party. "Bush is not Reagan," he wrote, "and really has no ideological agenda or consistent philosophical goals."[34]

The "Wimp" in Washington

After she returned from Washington, Nackey began to hear more grumblings from the right wing. The discontent intensified in 1990, when Bush reneged on his promise not to raise taxes and signed into law the Americans with Disabilities Act—a piece of legislation Nackey and her compatriots thought reeked of big government. (His decision to sign an updated civil rights act the following year lost Bush even more support among conservatives.) His foreign policy drew criticism too. The new president, Bablin wrote, "is too timid and cautious on the issue of freedom."[35] It didn't help matters that as the national jobless numbers grew, Bush spent weekends at his family's tony seaside compound on the coast of Maine.

Bush wondered privately if he should even seek a second term. His wife, according to many accounts of his presidency, was conflicted, too, and would have been happy if he'd returned to Texas after four years in the White House. Bush worried about how a second presidential campaign might affect his children, but his supporters—both hired staffers and blood relatives—convinced him to run again.[36] It would be a losing fight, and not just because he took his time making up his mind. As one retrospective of the 1992 campaigns notes, "Bush had the further bad luck to be seeking reelection at a time of deepening estrangement of the governed from the government. The divide was not a new one. . . . By 1992, it had been widening for 20 years. It had been glimpsed in the third-force candidacies of men as disparate as George Wallace in 1968 and John Anderson in 1980. It had boiled over in the tax revolt of the late 1970s. It had sent outsiders like Carter and Reagan to Washington with implicit mandates to clean house."[37]

From her vantage point in New Hampshire, Nackey sensed this antiestablishment wave and decided to help it grow by unleashing the power of her *Union Leader*. She knew she could rally support like she had four years before for Kirkpatrick, if she could find a true conservative willing to challenge Bush. It wouldn't be easy. Political history offers little encouragement for anyone seeking to topple an incumbent, but Nackey wasn't looking for a win. She was looking for an ideological war, one that would protect her version of conservatism and draw a new generation of followers into the movement. She focused her recruitment efforts on a person she'd long respected: Patrick Buchanan. She'd liked him from the moment he appeared on her snowy front steps at Prides Crossing all those years ago, and she'd watched his evolving career with interest. He was smart, a graduate of Washington DC's Gonzaga College High School, Georgetown University, and the Columbia School of Journalism. He'd worked for both Nixon and Reagan, and in between stints in the White House, he'd built a substantial following for his syndicated column.

Nackey also thought Buchanan would attract younger voters to the movement. He was still in his late forties at the end of Reagan's second term, when she first urged him to consider a presidential campaign. When he announced plans to speak at a fundraiser in New Hampshire in the spring of 1986, she promoted the event in a front-page editorial and encouraged readers to pay attention to what he had to say. "Americans have been deluged with semi-truths and opinions from a lot of people who don't really know what they are talking about," she wrote. "As a Washington-based columnist, TV and radio personality, [he] is in a position to know the facts."[38] On the day of his speech, she greeted Buchanan with another editorial encouraging him to return to New Hampshire soon. "This newspaper thinks it would be even nicer if he were to visit again—and for the same reason as the other political visitors. Looking at the present horde of hopefuls, we could do a lot worse."[39]

Her musings attracted the attention of other conservative publications, including *Human Events,* which in December 1986 published an article ("Pat Buchanan for President?") that named key conservatives intrigued by the idea of his candidacy. The list included a right-wing talk show host from California, a lawyer working for Senator Jesse Helms, and a rural newspaper publisher named Nackey Loeb. "While Buchanan's firm convictions and hard-knuckled rhetorical style are the things that have long made him the bête noire of the liberal media," the article proclaimed, "they are precisely the same things that make him a veritable hero figure on the right, fueling recent talk of his presidential hopes among some respected conservative leaders."[40]

The "Wimp" in Washington

Buchanan wouldn't enter the race in 1988, partly out of deference to the campaign of his friend Jack Kemp and partly out of fear that his candidacy would divide the conservative vote. Buchanan also wanted to focus on building his profile through his column, television appearances, and books. Although he declined to run, his name continued to surface among conservative activists unhappy with the state of the GOP. And he and Nackey stayed in touch. He had her home phone number and used it. She'd read Buchanan's latest book during one of her summer fishing trips; she especially liked the last few chapters where, she thought, he did a good job of summarizing a path forward for the country.[41] The *Union Leader* published his column, and Nackey quoted it often in her front-page editorials. She liked to give him advice too. "She was almost like a mom," Buchanan said, recalling how she'd encouraged him to sharpen his message. "Patrick, come on, be tougher. . . . I really liked her."[42]

At first Buchanan rebuffed her frequent suggestions of a presidential campaign, but he began to reconsider during the spring of 1990. His change of heart was motivated by frustrations with Bush's policy decisions, especially the tax increases.[43] He had his own political ambitions, of course, but like Nackey, he was also worried about the future of the right wing. He wrote to Nackey that April that he couldn't allow the Bush administration to "become permanently identified, in the eyes of the young, with our party and our movement. If we don't offer them an agenda of issues to debate, a platform on which to engage and battle liberalism, and a new fighting conservatism, we will lose the next generation to whatever young leader the Democrats produce. Though yours truly is carrying some rather embarrassing and unattractive scar tissue from a lot of old campaigns and White House battles . . . if no one better qualified to make the case against the Bushmen surfaces, I will take a hard look."[44]

Nackey kept pushing: "I think we have reached another crossroads," she wrote in June of 1990. "We are either going to stand up and fight to take back our country, or we will sit back and let the heathens take over."[45] A month later she nudged him again: "You could at least be the voice crying in the wilderness, heralding the Messiah for the true conservatives."[46]

Late in the fall of 1990, as the foliage on the hills outside her farm faded and the New Hampshire nights turned freezing cold, Nackey received a phone call from Buchanan. He was serious—really serious— about mounting a presidential campaign. Nackey's support would be crucial, and he wanted to hear her thoughts. "If Nackey Loeb and the *Union Leader* had been opposed to my running against George H. W. Bush, I would have wondered if . . . we really had any chance of doing well," Buchanan recalled. "It was . . . her encouragement to get in and her support that really sealed it for me."[47]

The two talked at length, and a few days later Nackey wrote him a letter. "I hope you don't wait too long," she said. "Right now, there are a lot of angry conservatives as well as just plain decent Americans who are looking for alternatives."[48]

The "Wimp" in Washington

Political Godmother 9

The timing *should* have been perfect. In early 1991 the New Hampshire GOP was hosting its annual fundraising dinner, and Buchanan agreed to give the keynote. His invitation to speak came from Governor Judd Gregg, who was frustrated that Bush seemed to be ignoring the Granite State. Putting Buchanan in front of a ballroom packed with local Republican power brokers might, the governor thought, help get the president's attention.[1] To Buchanan the evening represented a chance to test out his populist, isolationist message and gauge support in a state that would be crucial should he decide to run.

Nackey was ready to stir things up too. On the day of the speech, she published a front-page editorial that declared the 1992 primary officially under way. As evidence, she cited both Buchanan's visit and a speech Democrat Jesse Jackson planned to give later that week. Jackson got a passing mention. The rest of the editorial urged voters to consider Buchanan as more than a political commentator. "Pat Buchanan is a viable candidate," she wrote. "Through his columns and his television shows, he is a familiar name across the country, yet he has never been a vote-seeking politician. Perhaps the time has come for him to stop being the prophet and start being the leader." She also accused Bush of abandoning the Republican platform, predicted that his reelection was "no sure thing," and mentioned several other potential primary challengers, including DuPont and New Hampshire's Gordon Humphrey.[2]

Buchanan's speech hit a number of conservative high notes, decrying Bush for "accommodating the tree-hugger" by signing the Clean Air Act and criticizing his foreign policy, especially the build-up of troops in Kuwait. "It is time for a new foreign policy that looks out for America first, and not only America first but also America second and third," Buchanan said. "If Germany and Japan are big enough and tough enough to carry American markets in the world, they are big enough and tough enough to carry their own load in their own defense."[3] The message was a slam dunk for the right wing, and there were plenty of reporters on hand planning to write stories laced with speculation about Buchanan's candidacy. But thanks to a terrible coincidence, things didn't go as planned. While Buchanan talked, CNN began reporting that the United States and its allies were dropping bombs on Baghdad, heralding the start of the first Gulf War. This was before smartphones and push notifications, so Gregg had to take the stage and relay the news to the guests. He suspended party business, and the banquet hall began to empty. Buchanan, meanwhile, told the scrum of reporters that his political plans were no longer a subject for discussion. What mattered most, he said, was supporting the president and the troops deployed in support of the mission.

Nackey and the *Union Leader* pivoted too. The next day's paper carried a story about Buchanan's speech, but most of the news section was devoted to coverage of the war. Many members of New Hampshire's National Guard had been mobilized throughout the preceding year, and some of the largest units were based near Manchester. That made what was happening in the Middle East a local story for many in the *Union Leader*'s core communities. For several months the paper had been publishing a special military section that readers could clip and send to friends or relatives serving overseas. Nackey also arranged to have full issues of the paper mailed to local marines training at Camp Lejeune and encouraged readers to send mail to deployed service members.[4] For the most part, she suspended her editorials critical of the Bush administration. Instead, she unleased her patriotic populism on antiwar protesters and the news outlets she felt were giving them too much attention, instead of focusing on "the housewives wrapping parcels for the troops, or the school children writing letters, or . . . veterans marching behind the flag," she wrote. "But after all, these housewives, these children, these veterans are what America is all about. In spite of the racket from the rabble and the publicity it gets them, let us remember that and keep our priorities straight."[5]

Privately, Nackey held out hope that this wasn't the end of Buchanan's insurgency. She let both the potential candidate and members of his inner circle know he still had her support. "The President showed lousy timing in making his move at the same time, but I suppose we can't have everything," she wrote to Buchanan's sister Bay, who would become his campaign manager. "I hope that this platform makes for a good starting point, and I look forward to what the plans will be in the future. I am glad that you are by his side."[6] Nackey also continued to lobby on Buchanan's behalf. She arranged for him to speak at the New England Newspaper and Press Association's conference in Boston that spring and kept encouraging members of her letter-writing network—especially the well-connected conservative activists among them—to take a serious a look at his potential candidacy and tell their friends to do the same.[7]

By late February the first Gulf War was over; Bush seemed unbeatable to Republicans and Democrats alike. That began to change, though, as the summer wore on and the economy worsened. The president's approval rating sank, and Buchanan began once again to consider running. Nackey's support was an important factor, but he'd later say another major catalyst was Bush's decision to sign the Civil Rights Act of 1991—legislation he dismissed as a "quota bill." (The law was designed to provide more legal protections to victims of discrimination; Bush backed it as part of compromise with Democrats and other moderates after vetoing similar legislation the year before.) Buchanan also saw signs that the electorate was in the mood for a nontraditional candidate. He watched with interest when, in November 1991, Pennsylvania's Harris Wofford mounted a longshot campaign for a U.S. Senate seat in a special election and won. Wofford was a Democrat, but to Buchanan his victory hinted at the potential for unexpected outcomes.[8] Buchanan's mailbox, meanwhile, was full of letters from Nackey; many of them included messages from *Union*

Leader readers around the country who were eager to see someone upset the status quo.

That fall, Nackey took her recruitment effort public once again. In September 1991 she wrote one of her longest editorials, a 735-word argument in favor of Buchanan's America First formula. Among its highlights: withdrawing U.S. troops from the Korean peninsula, scaling back military alliances in Eastern Europe, making allies in the Pacific pay for U.S. military protection, and ending all foreign humanitarian and economic aid. To Nackey, such policies were the best path forward for the conservative movement. "We no longer have anticommunism as the binding force that had long-shaped our foreign policy," she wrote. "[Buchanan] reviews and rejects that vague concept of a New World Order, which would commit our sons to policing every piddling border dispute around the globe. Buchanan recognizes the failure of our political parties to rally support to their platforms—the Democrats with their concerns for special interest groups, and the Republican establishment with its concerns for the rest of the world. . . . America First was not and is not such a bad idea for this nation's survival."[9]

A few weeks before Thanksgiving 1991, Buchanan's campaign was beginning to take shape. It would never be a big operation, just a handful of paid staffers managed by Bay and a growing list of volunteers. But it would leave a lasting mark on the Republican Party and American politics. Buchanan focused on rallying support among his friends inside the Washington Beltway, holding a gathering at his house for what one book about the 1992 election called "the Lost Boys of the farther American right—the prophets, pamphleteers and activists whose access and influence had been sorely reduced since Ronald Reagan left town."[10] Bay, meanwhile, picked up the phone and called Nackey.

The two women had never met, and although they had exchanged a few notes by mail, Bay was still a little nervous about speaking to such a powerful figure. "I had such respect for her," Bay recalled. "I thought, oh, I'm going to talk to Nackey. This is kind of exciting." Nackey's unpre-

Political Godmother

tentious attitude put Bay immediately at ease, and they talked about the political landscape. Neither expected Buchanan to win, not in New Hampshire and certainly not nationally, but they agreed he was the best person to define the future of conservatism. Nackey didn't promise the *Union Leader*'s support right then, but Bay still viewed their talk as a success. "We felt invigorated," Bay said. "She didn't say 'are you nuts?' She didn't shut us down."[11] A few days later Nackey made her feelings about a Buchanan campaign even more clear. Under the headline "An NH Challenge for George Bush," she lamented that, come November, the only choice for Republicans might be to vote for Bush or stay home on Election Day.

> The conservative case needs to be made. Our current economic trouble, felt keenly right here in New Hampshire, is due to Bush's abandonment of the Reagan agenda of less government and lower taxes, which gave the nation unprecedented prosperity. The Democrats are making their case against Bush but no one, Bush included, is defending the conservative ideas and principles of the GOP.
>
> With 100 days left before the New Hampshire primary, nothing would serve the state or nation better than to have those principles defended, forcefully and with conviction. We know of no one better for that task than Pat Buchanan, longtime columnist for this newspaper and old friend of this publisher and conservatism. . . .
>
> Win or lose, that's the important thing to do. Run, Pat, run![12]

She mailed a copy to Buchanan, noting, "Now is the time to go for it if you are going to."[13] The editorial stopped short of endorsing Buchanan, but it gave his shoestring campaign a huge boost. "Pat was out of his mind," Bay recalls. "He was so excited."[14] The formal endorsement was almost anticlimactic, appearing in the *Union Leader* a little less than a month before the February 18 primary. "We were amazed this weekend to hear a knowledgeable media figure ask Editor-in-Chief Joe McQuaid who we would endorse for the presidency," Nackey wrote.

"We thought it was fairly obvious, but if they want us to make it official, here it is: *The Union Leader* endorses Pat Buchanan for President of the United States."[15]

Buchanan's base of support grew quickly, but he was far from an ideal candidate. He was, as one journalist put it, "burdened with more baggage than Imelda Marcos might have packed for August in Cannes."[16] In person he's charming—pleasant, funny, and full of great stories from his eclectic career in politics and media. But on the stump and in columns and television appearances, Buchanan's statements sent off warning bells across the ideological spectrum. *The New Republic* called his campaign a "repository of the darkest strains in American life: anxiety, intolerance, parochialism, fear."[17] *Newsweek* took issue with Buchanan's use of the America First slogan, pointing out that the original America First Committee was a group that, in the years before the United States entered World War II, advocated isolationist policies that were "also discernibly pro-German and anti-Semitic."[18] Another vocal critic of Buchanan was *New York Post* columnist Mike McAlary, who covered the New Hampshire primaries that year. He'd worked briefly in the *Union Leader*'s sports department, so he knew the state and the newspaper fairly well. "The relationship between Buchanan and the *Manchester Union Leader* borders on the pornographic," he wrote, calling Buchanan's campaign an "American nightmare" that told "people what they wanted to hear. . . . The president is a liar, Buchanan barked. It's okay to bash Japan. Go ahead and hate welfare recipients. America first and only."[19]

To Nackey, however, Buchannan was a true conservative and part of the solution to the many ideological battles—both social and geopolitical—she'd waged throughout her long career. At fifty-three, he was also fairly young, and Nackey thought he could help take the New Right of the 1970s into the twenty-first century. As primary day approached, Nackey defended her favored candidate, praising him for speaking his mind. "Pat Buchanan is a believer and a tough fighter," she wrote, "and certainly a man of conviction."[20]

Nackey had hoped to restart the *Union Leader Reader* newsletter ahead of the 1992 primary cycle, but it was hard to justify the cost given the poor economy. Instead, she worked to amplify her message in other ways, appearing on cable television and writing a steady stream of pro-Buchanan editorials designed to attract attention from out-of-state reporters covering the race. Her tactics worked. As primary day drew near and journalists arrived in New Hampshire by the dozens, everyone, it seemed, wanted to talk to Nackey. She was happy to oblige, taking frequent swipes at Bush. When C-SPAN's Brian Lamb asked her if there was anything the president could do to win her support, she replied, "Announce his retirement."[21]

On the day before the polls opened, Nackey made her closing argument on the front page of the *Union Leader*. "We think there is nothing wrong with being negative if our votes speak against the policies that are fast destroying the lives of American citizens," she wrote. "The most direct way to express disapproval of our incumbent president and the way things are is to vote for the man who is directly opposing him, namely Pat Buchanan. What's more, a vote for Buchanan is a vote for something—a return to the conservative principles George Bush preached but never practiced."[22]

Even without Buchanan's challenge to Bush, the 1992 New Hampshire primary would have been a doozy. Pride in the first Gulf War was fading fast, and the economy was in dreadful shape. While true-believer conservatives might have been looking to protest Bush's support of the Civil Rights Act of 1991, the Americans with Disabilities Act, and taxes, more mainstream voters were looking for salvation from layoffs and foreclosures. That was especially true in New Hampshire, where the recession had gutted the manufacturing sector. The Democratic field was large and fluid, with even the top-tier candidates vying for name recognition. (Bush's strong approval ratings after the Gulf War likely made many higher-profile candidates think twice about entering the race.) The Iowa caucuses had been formalities. No one challenged Bush on the Republican side. Democrats were unsurprised—and unenthusiastic—when Tom Harkin, a senator from the Hawkeye State, won handily. That made New Hampshire even more significant in 1992. Bill Clinton emerged as the Democratic frontrunner, with former Massachusetts senator Paul Tsongas close behind. That race grew tighter—and more tumultuous—when Clinton was accused of draft dodging, extramarital affairs, and sexual misconduct. Tsongas won New Hampshire with 33 percent of the vote, but Clinton salvaged his campaign by using his second-place finish with 25 percent of the vote to declare himself the "comeback kid."[23]

On the Republican side, the dynamics boiled down to what political scientists would later call "a classic protest vote."[24] Nackey used a different phrase to describe the race: "A real humdinger!"[25] As Buchanan's profile surged, Bush grew worried, and a few days before the primary, he made a swing through the state, shaking hands at a pancake breakfast and appearing at a local high school with Arnold Schwarzenegger. On C-SPAN, Nackey predicted that the last-minute trip would do little good; she also mocked him for calling on the former bodybuilder for support: "If Bush needs muscle . . ."[26] Still, Nackey didn't expect Buchanan to win. She'd view his campaign as a success if it earned 30 to 40 percent of the Republican vote—enough, in her mind, to shake up the conventional wisdom, rock the Bush campaign, and breathe new life into the conservative movement.[27]

When the polls closed on primary night, the race was tight—so tight that it briefly looked like Buchanan might win the state. Bush ended up first with 53 percent; when it came to the media narrative, though, Buchanan was victorious, earning 38 percent of the vote and dominating headlines in the next day's papers. Not all of his supporters were endorsing his strident conservatism, though. Polls would later find that fewer than a third of New Hampshire residents who voted for Buchanan did so because they actually wanted him to be president. The rest cast their ballots in protest of Bush's policies.[28]

The results of the race were good for Buchanan, who continued his campaign into other early voting states. Nackey's reputation benefited too. The same news outlets that had once characterized her as meek and predicted the *Union Leader*'s fall from national prominence were now paying close attention to what she had to say. She was amused at the change in tone. "Pity the dilemma of those 'spin doctors' who were saying a few weeks ago that the newspaper had lost its clout and are now saying the *Union Leader* gave Pat Buchanan the edge."[29] As the campaigns wore on, Nackey kept on boosting Buchanan, writing a half dozen favorable editorials. At one point she even suggested the GOP should replace Vice President Dan Quayle with Buchanan.[30] She offered him private encouragement too. "I wish you luck and an extra supply of energy during the next few months," she wrote. "No matter what the outcome, what is most important is the survival of conservatism and of the principles of the original Republican platform."[31]

Quayle stayed on the GOP ticket, Buchanan ended his campaign, and Nackey eventually endorsed Bush in the general election, saying he was imperfect but a far better choice than Clinton or third-party candidate Ross Perot. Buchanan may not have won the race, but he attracted enough support to earn an invitation to speak at the Republican National Convention in Houston. Modern political conventions are full of more bluster and pomp than real drama, but the featured speakers can hint at a party's ideological direction. Buchanan's address represented a rightward tack, one laced with both populist and socially conservative themes. His campaign had started with an isolationist message, but by the summer of 1992, he'd refocused his vision for the future of conservatism on social issues he believed could rally conservatives in a post–Cold War world. Buchanan thundered to the crowd packed into the Astrodome:

> Yes, we disagreed with President Bush, but we stand with him for the freedom to choose religious schools, and we stand with him against the amoral idea that gay and lesbian couples should have the same standing in law as married men and women. . . . We stand with President Bush for right-to-life and for voluntary prayer in the public schools. And we stand against putting our wives and daughters and sisters into combat units of the United States Army. . . . We stand with President Bush in favor of federal judges who interpret the law as written. . . . This election is about

more than who gets what. It is about who we are. It is about what we believe and what we stand for as Americans. There is a religious war going on in this country. It is a cultural war, as critical to the kind of nation we shall be as the Cold War itself. For this war is for the soul of America.[32]

Buchanan's speech delighted Republican delegates and shocked many Americans because of both its content and its fiery delivery. The reaction that followed was intense. Conservatives heralded the speech as a huge victory. Critics argued that it was bombastic and backward looking—a sentiment summarized by syndicated columnist Molly Ivins, who quipped that the speech "probably sounded better in the original German." Opinions about Buchanan's rhetoric differed, but it was clear that it was one of several factors that made the 1992 GOP convention a pivotal moment in American politics. It refocused the Republican base on social issues and fueled the culture wars that continue to shape political debate today.

It had been less than a year since Buchanan decided to mount a campaign; he was both thrilled and a little shocked at the opportunity to speak in Houston. He was also incredibly grateful to his friend, the New Hampshire newspaper publisher. Shortly before the convention, he suggested to the organizers that if Nackey was willing to make the trip to Texas, she would be the perfect person to warm up the crowd before he appeared. The Bush people flatly refused, saying, as Buchanan remembers it, "That's a bridge too far for the President."[33]

At some point during his campaign, Buchanan gave Nackey an America First bumper sticker. She placed it on her wheelchair and never took it off. The years after the 1992 primary were some of the busiest of Nackey's tenure as publisher. As the *Union Leader* was emerging from the recession and beginning to pay off debt related to the new plant, Nackey expanded her publishing footprint by buying a chain of weekly newspapers covering communities around Manchester. The local couple that had owned them for many years wanted to retire; Nackey worried that a big chain might snatch them up, something that would create new competition for the *Union Leader* and, in her opinion, be bad for readers. The weeklies were completely different from her other newspapers. Nackey saw running the *Union Leader* as a duty, but as her older daughter Nackey Scagliotti remembers it, she thought her new weeklies were "loads of fun" and that they made her feel more connected to daily life. "She viewed them as an essential part of small-town life," Scagliotti recalls. "She delighted in designing the logo, loved talking with the editor about the importance of publishing school lunch menus, covering town hall meetings, and reporting on 4H events."[34]

She wrote fewer front-page editorials for the *Union Leader* during the mid-1990s, but her profile was higher than ever before. In 1993 a local magazine named her "Most Powerful Woman in New Hampshire," and conservatives from around the country sought her counsel. She also continued to follow—and attempt to shape—national politics. Like many conservatives, she was dismayed by the Clinton administration, dismissing the president and his wife as "Billary" and accusing the "liberal media" of intentionally waiting until after his inauguration to start reporting good news about the economy. But she also saw the Clintons as a long-term opportunity for right-wing Republicans to engage a new generation of activists. She'd seen it happen before, during the years when the *Union Leader* backed Goldwater. His campaign failed, but his legacy endured. "The original Goldwater kids on college campuses who rallied to him became the adults who supported Ronald Reagan and, for a while at least, made conservatism a reality," Nackey wrote to a friend in 1993. "Now, I suspect that there will be such a reaction against Clinton that once more conservatives will be able to come out on top if they can only find the leadership and if they can stop squabbling among themselves."[35]

Nackey and Buchanan remained in touch and began discussing the idea that he should run again. In late 1994 three Buchanans arrived at Nackey's farm: Pat, Bay, and Pat's wife, Shelley. He wasn't the only potential candidate to come calling that fall, and Nackey made no promises to the Buchanan contingent about an endorsement. She wrote to him soon after, though, about her disappointment with the rest of the emerging field. "I see no one who has the Ronald Reagan quality of inspiring the voters," she lamented. "I suppose the qualities of leadership and trust are the ones that will count if we want to clean out the house."[36] She was, however, buoyed by the Republicans' success in the 1994 midterms, when the Contract with America helped the party win the House, the Senate, and a number of gubernatorial races. In her mind, Buchanan's voice would help build on that success, but she wasn't thinking just about 1996. She was hoping to plant ideas in the electorate that might not yield results for one or even two decades to come. "We have been many years fighting in the same army for the same cause," she wrote to him in the spring of 1995. "There will be more years to come."[37]

On the day Buchanan launched his 1996 presidential campaign, Nackey was among the first people C-SPAN called for comment. It was a quick conversation, and the *Union Leader* had yet to issue its endorsement, but Nackey's enthusiasm was unmistakable. "Last time around, [Buchanan] was sort of a lone voice in the wilderness," she said. "I think it's less so this time around. More people are beginning to realize that there's always something to what Pat fought for. I have been watching this wind of change all across the country . . . and the most important change is the participation of the public, taking back their control and their power."[38]

The *Union Leader* officially backed Buchanan a second time in September 1995—an unusually early endorsement, even considering the ever-expanding election cycle—but Nackey thought it would help him debunk a narrative that his campaign could never succeed. It would turn out to be Nackey's last primary, and her performance was memorable. When it came to supporting Buchanan, she pulled out all the stops, at one point appearing on C-SPAN wearing a maroon sweater, a floral scarf, and a Buchanan campaign button pinned over her heart. As political scientists would later determine, the *Union Leader* did a lot more than just issue an endorsement to support Buchanan. A systematic analysis of the newspaper's content found a connection between extensive and largely positive coverage of Buchanan and his performance in tracking polls. In editorials, op-ed columns, and news stories, the paper was far more likely to publish positive news about Buchanan than it was about the other major candidates running that year. When it came to negative coverage, the inverse was true; Bob Dole, Lamar Alexander, and Steve Forbes received more negative coverage than Buchanan.[39] "Without the newspaper's editorial support and biased coverage in its news columns, Bob Dole would almost certainly have won the primary, and it's very likely that Lamar Alexander would have come in second—producing a very different political context from the one that actually occurred."[40]

When the polls closed on primary night, the early returns showed a tight race between Buchanan and the establishment favorite, Dole. It took hours for the vote totals to finish rolling in, but Buchanan finally eked out a win with 27 percent of the vote, just a single point ahead of Dole. It was an upset that, as the *Boston Globe* put it, "shattered the Republican field" by "riding a wave of support from religious conservatives and anxious blue-collar workers."[41] At a predawn victory party in Manchester, Buchanan described the outcome as a win not just for him but for the conservative movement. He made it clear to the crowd that he'd had help along the way, thanking all of his local volunteers and the newspaper that had supported him for so long. "My heart is filled with gratitude for another person tonight, Nackey Loeb," he said. "Nackey Loeb is the political godmother of Pat Buchanan. Without her fighting *Union Leader* . . . we would not be here tonight."[42]

It was a late night for Nackey, too, as she watched the returns from her farm. As soon as the race was called for Buchanan, C-SPAN got Nackey on the phone. The anchor was Susan Swain, one of the journalists who had documented Nackey's first primary as publisher a dozen years before. She smiled broadly when the older woman's voice came through on the phone.

"Your man won," said Swain. "What's your reaction?"

"My man won," Nackey replied, sounding a little amazed. "This has been a pretty heady evening. . . . I am thrilled."

Swain then asked her if she took any credit for Buchanan's victory.

"I don't know," Nackey replied. "It's pretty hard to pin down from where I sit. . . . I would hope that we made some impression on our readers."[43]

Conclusion

Nackey's final front-page editorial appeared on February 18, 1999. There was no farewell. No reminiscing. It's unclear if she even knew the column would be her last, but it was among her most biting. President Bill Clinton's impeachment trial had ended the week before, and he was visiting New Hampshire to attempt to repair his battered public image in a state that had been friendly territory for nearly a decade. When he arrived, local Democrats greeted him warmly. Nackey, unsurprisingly, did not. On the front page of her newspaper, she unleashed a no-holds-barred takedown, calling him a "disgrace" and suggesting he resign. "Even when it was purely political, it was something special just to have the President of our country in our midst," she wrote. "Not anymore. Not today. Not with this man. . . . The sooner he leaves New Hampshire, the better."[1]

The editorial attracted nationwide attention. Newspapers in dozens of states reprinted an Associated Press story that quoted it liberally. A column in the *Boston Globe* called Nackey's rhetoric "venomous."[2] During the following weeks, letters and emails from readers arrived by the dozen. Most agreed with Nackey's sentiment, but she also heard from critics who thought she was being too harsh. McQuaid, who had assumed more management duties during the late 1990s, handled most of the responses, signing stacks of polite form letters thanking readers for sharing their opinions.[3]

Three months later, Nackey resigned as publisher and president of the Union Leader Corporation, naming McQuaid as her successor. She tried to leave quietly, skipping a formal sendoff and instead sending thank-you notes to loyal employees. But her retirement sparked widespread speculation about the future of the *Union Leader* and the effect her departure might have on the 2000 presidential primary. It also disappointed her still-growing network of fans. In one of her final major business decisions, Nackey convinced her managers to expand the *Union Leader* onto the newly popular World Wide Web. The paper's digital debut came shortly after the 1996 elections and quickly earned Nackey a fresh following. Soon after the website launched, the newsroom's general email address received a slew of notes from happy conservatives. Many of them were addressed to Nackey. "Keep up your fine newspaper even if the liberals make fun of you," wrote one new reader. "Thanks for your courage and integrity. You keep, at least in my mind, a light of hope that we will not go the way of the Roman Empire." Not all of the email was adoring (one writer called Nackey "senile" and said it was frightening she was allowed to run a newspaper), but the overall response showed that, once again, Nackey had forged new connections with an audience hungry for right-wing news sources.[4]

At the time of her retirement, Nackey was seventy-five years old and dealing with a host of health challenges, most of them related to the injuries she'd sustained in the Jeep accident that left her paralyzed. She'd also been diagnosed with skin cancer and in 1998 had surgery to remove a worrisome spot on her scalp. She remained in characteristically good spirits, writing a lighthearted editorial that encouraged readers to wear sunscreen and assuring them that she was on the mend. "Though I have been accused before of having a hole in my head," she wrote, "I can certify that I don't, thanks to good medical care."[5] It was a challenging time in many ways, and one of Nackey's chief concerns was the future of the *Union Leader*. She feared her death would mean the end of local ownership, something she thought would be bad for the paper's employees and the audiences it served.

As her health declined, her older daughter, Nackey Scagliotti, became her caregiver and business partner, serving as assistant publisher of both the *Union Leader* and the chain of weeklies the elder Nackey acquired in the early 1990s. (Nackey's younger daughter, Edith

Tomasko, preferred horses to newspapers and turned part of the family's farm into a nonprofit therapeutic riding center that continues to operate today.) The two women worked together closely during that time, and Scagliotti recalls that her mother talked often about the future of the *Union Leader*. Nackey feared that if the paper were to pass to her heirs, they might someday be forced to sell it to a chain to cover the cost of inheritance taxes. While researching different business models, they learned about the Poynter Institute, a nonprofit training academy in Florida that has owned the *Tampa Bay Times* since the late 1970s. Nackey wondered if a similar arrangement could protect the *Union Leader* while also addressing another of her worries—a lack of knowledge among teenagers about the First Amendment and other aspects of civic life. In collaboration with her daughters and McQuaid, Nackey created the nonprofit Nackey S. Loeb School of Communications in Manchester.[6] Just like Poynter owns the *Tampa Bay Times*, the Loeb School owns the majority of the Union Leader Corporation.[7] And since its opening in 1999, the school has offered frequent free or low-cost workshops on writing, photography, digital storytelling, media law, cartooning, and more.

Nackey died at the age of seventy-five on January 8, 2000, just a few weeks before that year's New Hampshire primary. While she was ill, McQuaid sought her opinion on the field of Republican candidates, and with her blessing the *Union Leader* endorsed Steve Forbes. Her death was international news, and her funeral was broadcast on c-span. Inside a packed Manchester church, neighbors, children, and grandchildren shared pews with political power brokers from several generations. They all remembered her fondly for her generosity, her humor, and her political influence. Buchanan—at that point a presidential candidate for the Reform Party—sat near Forbes. After the service, he spoke to reporters about the impact that his longtime friend the newspaper publisher had on the conservative movement.

"Without Nackey Loeb, we simply would not be where we are today," Buchanan said. "She was indispensable . . . a rocklike figure in a gentle way."[8]

Today's *Union Leader* is not Nackey Loeb's *Union Leader*. Journalism—especially political journalism—is different. And running a newspaper is harder than ever before. The modern *Union Leader* reflects those realities. It still operates out of the building Nackey planned on the outskirts of Manchester, but now it's a tenant, having sold the property in 2017 to a commercial real estate investor. The newsroom is smaller than it used to be in terms of both physical size and staff, but on one afternoon a few days before Christmas 2018 it was bustling with editors and reporters frontloading production ahead of the holiday. A tree twinkled near one end of the room. Stockings hung on the reception desk. A table was covered with the remnants of an office potluck, and poinsettias overflowed from the corners. It felt very much like a family business, in part because it still is. As of early 2019, McQuaid continued to serve as publisher and write regular editorials. Both of his children also held leadership roles at the time, his daughter Katie as vice president of business development and his son Brendan as president of the Union Leader Corporation. (Scagliotti served on the company's board of directors until 2008. The weekly papers she led after her mother's death were eventually merged into the Union Leader Corporation and continue to operate today.)

The modern *Union Leader* has its critics and its fans, but it remains independently owned, editorially spunky, and intensely focused on life in New Hampshire. On the editorial page, the *Union Leader* endures as a conservative stalwart, and its opinion writers still know how to make a splash—something McQuaid demonstrated during the 2016 primary when he feuded openly with then-candidate Donald Trump. The paper's candidate of choice that year was New Jersey governor Chris Christie, a fairly routine endorsement that didn't do much to help Christie, who came in sixth with 7 percent of the vote. Donald Trump won New Hampshire handily with 35 percent of the Republican vote, nearly twenty points ahead of second place finisher John Kasich of Ohio. About a month after the primary, though, McQuaid attracted national attention when he retracted the paper's endorsement of Christie after he dropped out of the race and backed Donald Trump.

"Rather than stand up to the bully," McQuaid wrote, "Christie bent his knee. In doing so, he rejected the very principles of his campaign that attracted our support." McQuaid remained so troubled by Trump—who has called the *Union Leader* both "dishonest" and "failing"—that in the general election the paper broke with a hundred years of tradition and didn't endorse the Republican presidential nominee.[9] Instead, it supported Libertarian Gary Johnson. The move earned applause from the never-Trump camp, but Johnson received only 4 percent of the vote in New Hampshire. (Hillary Clinton won the state, but it was a narrow victory. She pulled in just under 48 percent, less than half a point ahead of Trump.)

Between presidential primaries, the *Union Leader* is a lot like any local news organization. Its journalists cover town council meetings, tweet breaking news, and file right-to-know requests. They report from the sidelines at high school sports arenas, identify business trends, and dig up quirky feature stories. Like all newspapers, the *Union Leader* faces serious business challenges, but decisions about its future will be made by people with deep roots in the local community. In that way, Nackey's many years as publisher and the business decisions she made at the end of her life have had a lasting impact on local journalism in New Hampshire.

Her ideological legacy is harder to measure. Nackey didn't create right-wing populism—no single person or media entity did—but she played a crucial role in amplifying aspects of its message and connecting its adherents, hinting at the power and divisive rhetoric that results when fellow travelers find new ways to interact with each other. During her life, though, Nackey believed her approach to audience engagement would bring people together in civic debate, not send them scurrying apart into ideological bunkers. She had strong, sometimes controversial opinions and used her newspaper to share them. At the same time, the *Union Leader*'s expansive letters pages allowed regular people, even those who disagreed with her, to have their say too. She could not have predicted today's highly fractured political climate, but her sprawling audience of malcontents helps explain the deep roots of the antiestablishment enthusiasm that propelled Trump to the White House.

Buchanan once said that "the conservative movement has always advanced from its defeats."[10] Perhaps that statement is a useful way to look at the lasting impact of both his career and Nackey's. His campaigns failed, but much of his rhetoric endured. Similarly, her behind-the-scenes activism and editorial crusades weren't always successful, at least in the short term. But that wasn't really her goal. Nackey was, in many ways, playing the long game, preserving the message of the right wing until a new generation was ready to hear it.

During the two years I've spent writing this book, I've pondered what Nackey would think of the Trump presidency. I'm still not sure. As many people have pointed out, there are numerous parallels between Trump's rhetoric and Buchanan's, but they are very different men who launched campaigns in very different times. Trump has also been compared to Nixon. The *Union Leader* tried to unseat Nixon by endorsing a primary challenger during his 1972 reelection campaign, but it later issued a tepid endorsement in the general election. It's possible that Nackey, like many on the right, would have viewed Trump as a flawed but strategically important candidate who could infuse the courts, the White House, and other corners of the federal government with conservative ideology. Given her history, though, it's also possible she would have applauded McQuaid's unconventional choice to back Libertarian Gary Johnson. Or maybe she would have tried once again to recruit a candidate of her own.

As I write this, New Hampshire's 2020 primary is still nine long, unpredictable months away. The political landscape is drastically different than it was in Nackey's day, and not just because Trump is in the White House. The *Union Leader* faces stiff competition both locally and nationally from news organizations using a dizzying array of digital platforms to attract eyeballs and attempt to influence political debate. The only prediction I will make about 2020 is that the staff of the *Union Leader* will work hard to provide coverage and commentary about what's sure to be a fascinating and grueling election cycle. I also find

Conclusion

myself wondering what Nackey would think about blogs, Twitter, and other aspects of the digital media ecosystem. Somehow I can't imagine her tweeting, but I suspect that her chatty editorial style would have translated well to the blogosphere. I do know, however, that she would have plenty to say. And no matter what medium she picked to deliver her message, her audience would, as always, be waiting.

Notes

INTRODUCTION

1. "New Hampshire Primary and DuPont Endorsement," C-SPAN, February 13, 1988.
2. Patrick Buchanan, "1996 Victory Speech—Manchester, NH," Patrick J. Buchanan Official Website, February 20, 1996, https://buchanan.org/blog/1996-victory -speech-manchester-nh-183.
3. Steve Dunleavy, "Voice from the Grave Cries out for Forbes," *New York Post*, January 26, 2000, 6; "Nackey Loeb Dies," *Washington Post*, January 9, 2000.
4. Julia Ioffe, "Meet the New Hampshire Newspaper Publisher Who's at War with Donald Trump," *Washington Post*, January 21, 2016.
5. "Tribute to William Loeb," C-SPAN, December 11, 1985.
6. "Scripps' Kin Rips Papers' M'Carthy Views," *Chicago Daily Tribune*, July 17, 1954.
7. Tom Muller, "Yankee Publisher Friend to South," *The Citizen*, December 1972.
8. For more on the roots of conservative media, see Hemmer, *Messengers of the Right*.
9. Nackey Scripps Loeb to Clayton Brown, July 20, 1993, ULC. Nackey wrote that she and William Loeb worried that competing publishers might "be eager to snatch up *The Union Leader* if it were to become available. For that reason, the situation was hush-hush, and many of the letters during the last period had his signature but were written by me."
10. "Union Leader," C-SPAN, February 21, 1984.
11. Nackey Scagliotti, email interview with the author, January 29, 2019.
12. Greg Sullivan, telephone interview with the author, February 28, 2019.
13. Tuchman, "Annihilation of Women by the Mass Media."
14. Beasley, "Study of Women's History in American Journalism," 209. Beasley argues for a broader, more inclusive definition of journalism, one that acknowledges "the historical constraints, limitations and opportunities available to women in journalism."

1. Veblen, *The Manchester "Union Leader."*

2. "Citizen Loeb," *60 Minutes*, February 1, 1976, CBS.

3. "Washington Sunday Journal," C-SPAN, February 20, 1996.

4. For instance, Nackey Loeb, "She Knows Who She Is, Where She's Going," *New Hampshire Sunday News*, January 27, 1980.

5. United Press International, "Bush Courts Right Wing at Fundraiser," *Arizona Republic*, December 12, 1985.

6. Nackey Scripps Loeb, "Justice for Max Hugel," *Union Leader*, November 18, 1981.

7. Nackey Scripps Loeb, "King John and the GOP," *Union Leader*, January 15, 1985.

8. Michael Kranish, "Bush to Honor His Late Critic," *Boston Globe*, December 1, 1985.

9. Michael Kranish, "Bush to Honor His Late Critic," *Boston Globe*, December 1, 1985.

10. Nackey Scripps Loeb to Clayton Brown, November 2, 1986, ULC.

11. Walter V. Robinson, "Bush Honors an Old Foe—Loeb," *Boston Globe*, December 12, 1985; Germond and Witcover, *Mad as Hell*, 20–22.

12. Nackey Scripps Loeb to George H. W. Bush, November 27, 1985, ULC.

13. Nackey Scripps Loeb to Clayton Brown, November 2, 1986, ULC.

14. Nackey Scripps Loeb to Joseph Elia, January 2, 1986, ULC.

15. "Tribute to William Loeb," C-SPAN, December 11, 1985.

16. "Tribute to William Loeb," C-SPAN, December 11, 1985.

17. For instance, Tracy Everbach, "The Culture of a Women-Led Newspaper: An Ethnographic Study of the Sarasota Herald-Tribune"; and Joe Strupp, "Breaking Through," *MediaWeek*, November 3, 2003.

18. Dudley Clendinen, "Loeb's Paper Serves New Hampshire Less Venom," *New York Times*, September 30, 1982.

19. Brad Pokorny, "The *Union Leader* 'Will Live' . . . But Will It Still Pack a Punch?," *Boston Globe*, September 18, 1981.

20. Dudley Clendinen, "New Hampshire Ponders Future Without Powerful Conservative Publisher," *New York Times*, September 18, 1981.

21. Joe McQuaid, "Nackey S. Loeb Assures Her Pledge Is Kept," *Union Leader*, September 13, 1982.

22. Nackey Scripps Loeb, "What Now? Bill Loeb Will Live Because the Union Leader Will Live," *Union Leader*, September 15, 1981.

23. "A Paper's a Public Servant, Mrs. Loeb Tells Press Club," *Union Leader*, November 19, 1982.

24. "Loeb Newspapers Are 'Alive and Well,'" *Union Leader*, April 20, 1982.

25. "Mrs. Loeb Will Maintain Tradition of Newspapers," *New Hampshire Sunday News*, February 7, 1982.

26. Heckman, "Needle, Not Sword."

27. For instance, FedEx receipts for packages sent to the White House, December 19, 1986, and January 27, 1987, ULC.

28. Ronald Reagan to Nackey Scripps Loeb, Manchester NH, May 5, 1984, ULC.

29. Skinner, Anderson, and Anderson, *Reagan: A Life in Letters*.

30. Nackey Scripps Loeb, "Letter to the President: What's Going on Here?," *Union Leader*, January 19, 1983.

31. Moore and Smith, *First Primary*, 78; Sprague, "The New Hampshire Primary." Nixon won the 1972 New Hampshire primary with 68 percent of the vote. California representative Pete McCloskey came in second with 20 percent. Ashbrook finished third with 10 percent.

32. Veblen, *The Manchester "Union Leader."*

33. Benjamin Taylor, "Reagan Touts High Tech in Boston: Questions Corporate Income Tax," *Boston Globe*, January 27, 1983; Irene Sege, "Protests, Yes, But There Was Cheering, Too," *Boston Globe*, January 27, 1983.

34. See, for instance, Robert M. Mackay, "Reagan Campaign to Let Reagan Be Reagan," UPI, October 11, 1984.

35. Joe McQuaid, interview with the author, December 22, 2018, Manchester NH; Nackey Scripps Loeb to Gordon Rogers, Kingston GA, February 16, 1983, ULC.

36. Nackey Scripps Loeb to Charles Scripps, Cincinnati, February 15, 1983, ULC.

37. Robert Turner, "Mrs. Loeb Maintains Union Leader's Clout," *Boston Globe*, February 3, 1983.

38. "Election Review," *C-SPAN Update*, March 4, 1984.

39. Susan Swain. "In New Hampshire, the Electricity Is on the Air and Off," *C-SPAN Update*, March 4, 1984.

40. "A Day in the Life of the *Union Leader*," C-SPAN, February 21, 1984.

41. Brian Lamb, telephone interview with the author, September 6, 2018.

42. "New Hampshire Primary," C-SPAN, February 24, 1984.

43. "New Hampshire Primary," C-SPAN, February 24, 1984.

44. Union Leader Corporation, internal memo, March 14, 1984, ULC. According to an interview McQuaid gave to C-SPAN in February 1984, the *Union Leader* had about three thousand out-of-state subscribers before that year's primary.

45. Union Leader Corporation, internal memo, February 27, 1984, ULC.

1. E. W. Scripps died at the age of seventy-one on March 12, 1926, while sailing aboard his yacht, the *Ohio*. He was buried at sea off the coast of Liberia.

2. "Robert P. Scripps Dies on His Yacht," *New York Times*, March 4, 1938. For more on Bob Scripps's rise to the top of the Scripps-Howard concern, see Casserly, *Divided Dynasty*.

3. Nackey Scripps Loeb, "A New Year's Message," *Union Leader*, December 31, 1992.

4. "Brunch and Politics in New Hampshire," C-SPAN, February 16, 1992; Nackey Scagliotti, email interview with the author, January 2019.

5. Baldasty, *E. W. Scripps*, 1.

6. Baldasty, *E. W. Scripps*, 2.

7. Baldasty, *E. W. Scripps*, 1–5.

8. Sheehy, "Capitalism as Necessary Evil."

9. Casserly, *Divided Dynasty*, 16–22; biographical note, E. W. Scripps papers, EWSC.

10. Biographical note, E. W. Scripps papers, EWSC.

11. Casserly, *Divided Dynasty*; "Robert P. Scripps Dies on His Yacht," *New York Times*, March 4, 1938.

12. "Robert P. Scripps Dies on His Yacht," *New York Times*, March 4, 1938.

13. E. W. Scripps to Robert Paine Scripps, May 8, 1912, series 1.2, box 18, folder 10, EWSC.

14. Casserly, *Divided Dynasty*, 34.

15. Elizabeth Anne Scripps, certificate of live birth, Los Angeles County Clerk's Office. Informational copy provided to author on August 30, 2018.

16. Telegram, Robert Paine Scripps to E. W. Scripps at sea, February 24, 1924, series 1.2, box 27, folder 5, EWSC.

17. E. W. Scripps to Ellen Browning Scripps, June 9, 1924, series 1.2, box 25, folder 8, EWSC.

18. Robert Paine Scripps to E. W. Scripps, April 21, 1920, series 1.1, box 38, folder 6, EWSC; Nackey Scripps Loeb to Charles Rudolph, Ridgefield CT, July 24, 1989; Nackey Scripps Loeb to Harold Biggar, Ridgefield CT, August 10, 1987, ULC.

19. Nackey Scagliotti, email interview with the author, January 2019.

20. "Robert P. Scripps Dies on His Yacht," *New York Times*, March 4, 1938.

21. Nackey Scagliotti, email interview with the author, January 2019.

22. Adams, "Josephine Scripps."

23. Nackey Scripps Loeb to Edward Fike, El Cajon CA, June 2, 1992, ULC.

24. Biographical note, E. W. Scripps papers, EWSC.

25. McClain, *Ellen Browning Scripps*.

26. Nackey Scripps to Edward Fike, San Diego, November 8, 1988, ULC.

27. Nackey Scagliotti, email interview with the author, January 2019; Nackey Scripps Loeb to James W. Hendrick, Oklahoma City, October 27, 1986, ULC.

28. Nackey Scripps Loeb to Bob Scripps, July 25, 1996, ULC.

29. The Bishop's School was founded in 1909 by Ellen Browning Scripps and her half sister, Virginia. It continues to operate today as a coeducational day school.

30. Nackey Scripps Loeb to Joseph and Clara Elia, Reno, January 3, 1986, ULC.

31. "Robert P. Scripps Dies on His Yacht," *New York Times*, March 4, 1938.

32. "Robert P. Scripps Dies on His Yacht," *New York Times*, March 4, 1938; United Press International, "Robert P. Scripps Dies on Yacht Trip," *Pittsburgh Press*, March 4, 1938; "Scripps-Howard Boss Weds Widow of Scripps," *Montgomery Advertiser*, October 24, 1943. At the time of his death, Bob Scripps was in charge of twenty-five newspapers.

33. Casserly, *Divided Dynasty*, 73; Gallowhur v. Gallowhur, Windsor County Court, Windsor VT, August 1949, VSA.

34. Kaiser, *Gay Metropolis*, 7–12.

35. "Sun, Bugs and Mold," *Time*, September 6, 1943.

36. See Kaiser's *Gay Metropolis* for more on the complexities of gay life during the first half of the twentieth century.

37. Marriage certificate of George Gallowhur and Nackey E. Scripps, Clerk's Office, Clark County, Nevada. Certified copy provided to author on August 17, 2018. They were married on October 27, 1944.

38. "Prominent Couple Now Honeymooning at Desert Inn," *Desert Sun*, November 10, 1944; "Miss Scripps Goes to Alter," *Los Angeles Times*, October 28, 1944.

39. Gallowhur v. Gallowhur, VSA; "Hubby Faces Counter Suit: Wife Says Spouse Spent Her Money," *Windsor (ON) Star*, August 15, 1949; "Matco Foresees Great Expansion Here Under Tie-up with Large Chemical Co.," *Burlington (VT) Free Press*, August 11, 1945.

40. Cash, *Who the Hell Is William Loeb?*, 102.

41. Gfroerer, NHPBS *Presents: Powerful as the Truth*. Others on the list included John D. Rockefeller, Henry Ford, and William Randolph Hearst.

42. Gfroerer, NHPBS *Presents: Powerful as the Truth*, 05:52.

43. Gfroerer, NHPBS *Presents: Powerful as the Truth*.

44. "Union Leader," C-SPAN, February 21, 1984.

45. Cash, *Who the Hell Is William Loeb?*, 159.

46. Gfroerer, NHPBS *Presents: Powerful as the Truth*.

47. The executives were Bernard Victor and Joseph Ridder.

48. Gfroerer, NHPBS Presents: Powerful as the Truth; Clark, "Newspapering in New Hampshire." Clark appreciated McQuaid's energy but quickly grew frustrated with his temper and bought him out in 1947. A couple of weeks later, Loeb hired McQuaid in the editorial department of the *Union Leader* and the two began making plans to buy the *Sunday News*, which they did in the fall of 1948.

49. Cash, *Who the Hell Is William Loeb?*, 180–81; Wolfgang Saxon, "William Loeb Is Dead at 75; Owned Conservative Papers," *New York Times*, September 14, 1981.

50. "Union Leader," C-SPAN, February 21, 1984.

51. Cash, *Who the Hell Is William Loeb?*, 139; Clark, "Newspapering in New Hampshire." For more on E. W. Scripps's progressive tendencies, see Baldasty's *E. W. Scripps* and Sheehy's "Capitalism as Necessary Evil."

52. Penny Loeb went on to become a successful and award-winning investigative journalist and author. In 1989 she was a finalist for the Pulitzer Prize in investigative reporting for her stories revealing that well-off New Yorkers were living in subsidized housing. For more, see https://www.pulitzer.org/finalists/penny-loeb.

53. Cash, *Who the Hell Is William Loeb?*, 159; Roy Howard to Nackey Gallowhur, Burlington VT, July 19, 1950, RWH; Gallowhur v. Gallowhur, VSA.

54. "Publisher Is Sued in Love Balm Action," *Rutland (VT) Daily Herald*, August 8, 1949.

55. "Cross Libel Is Served on Gallowhur: Scripps Heiress Accuses Reading Man of Intolerable Severity, Non-Support," *Rutland (VT) Daily Herald*, August 16, 1949, 1.

56. "Hubby Faces Count Suit: Wife Says Spouse Spent Her Money," *Windsor (ON) Star*, August 15, 1949, 19.

57. Gallowhur v. Gallowhur, deposition of Dr. Frank H. Everett, Rutland VT, VSA.

58. Certificate of divorce, December 1, 1949, VSA. George Gallowhur later remarried and had a son. He died in March 1974 at the age of sixty-nine in Miami, where he'd worked for fifteen years at the Biscayne Chemical Corporation.

59. Reno Divorce History, www.renodivorcehistory.org/themes/law-of-the-land; "Decrees Granted," *Nevada State Journal* (Reno), July 12, 1952.

60. Penny Loeb, telephone interview with the author, January 4, 2019; "Divorce Valid," *Bridgeport (CT) Post*, May 4, 1955, 116.

61. "Newspaper Couple Wed at Reno Church," *Reno Gazette*, July 16, 1952.

62. Nackey Scripps Loeb to Joseph Elia, September 11, 1989, ULC.

3. "ROTTEN, BIASED JOURNALISM"

1. "William Loeb and Nackey Scripps of Newspaper Chain Family to Wed Soon," *Burlington (VT) Free Press*, July 15, 1952. Loeb's divorce was granted by default because his second wife failed to answer the complaint.

2. The Loebs owned the ranch house and other structures on the property but leased the land from a rancher named Henry Heidenreich.

3. "Meetings Planned by Mt. Rose P-TA," *Nevada State Journal*, September 18, 1954, 1.

4. "Around the Town," *Nashua Telegraph*, July 15, 1954; Penny Loeb, telephone interview with the author, January 4, 2019; Nackey Scagliotti, email interview with the author, January 2019.

5. Glenn Wallace, "With a Picture Perfect Move, the Paper Never Missed a Beat," *Union Leader*, August 27, 1990.

6. Nackey Scripps Loeb to Alyn Denham, May 5, 1986, ULC; Nackey Gallowhur to Roy Howard, New York City, March 31, 1952, and Roy Howard to Nackey Gallowhur, Manchester NH, April 8, 1952, RWH. A series of letters between Nackey and Howard document how, shortly after her divorce, she attempted to broker a potentially lucrative newsprint deal between William Loeb's newspapers and Scripps-Howard. Her plan never came to fruition, with Howard citing an overabundance of newsprint.

7. Ann Marie Williams, "There Is Nothing So Powerful as Nackey S. Loeb," *Manchester/Concord Business Digest*, June 1985.

8. Dennis Tristram, "Publisher Loeb Still Believes in Absolutes," *Nevada State Journal*, October 19, 1975.

9. "Citizen Loeb," *60 Minutes*, February 1, 1976, CBS.

10. Dennis Tristram, "Publisher Loeb Still Believes in Absolutes," *Nevada State Journal*, October 19, 1975; "New Hampshire Conservative Publisher Loeb Terms Muskie a Phony, Then Adds Nixon to the Same List," *Courier-Journal* (Louisville KY), March 2, 1972; photo of Nackey Scripps Loeb with Richard Nixon, n.d., ULC; assorted photos of Nackey Scripps Loeb at *Union Leader* community events, n.d., ULC; photo of Nackey Scripps Loeb, William Loeb, and others holding awards, April 16, 1977, box 1015936232, "Loeb, William," BGLC.

11. "About McCarthy," *Time*, July 19, 1954.

12. Frederick Woltman, "The McCarthy Balance Sheet, Part Two," *New Work World-Tribune*, July 13, 1954.

13. "Scripps' Kin Rips Papers' M'Carthy Views," *Chicago Daily Tribune*, July 17, 1954.

14. "Woltman V. McCarthy," *Time*, August 2, 1954.

15. "Union Leader," C-SPAN, February 24, 1984.

16. Jodie T. Allen, "How a Different America Responded to the Great Depression," Pew Research Center, December 14, 2010.

17. Lora and Longton, *Conservative Press*, 10–15.

18. Robert P. Scripps obituary, *Corpus-Christi (TX) Caller-Times*, October 24, 2012.

19. "Heirs Lose in Plea for Income," *Cincinnati Enquirer*, December 17, 1950.

20. McGirr, *Suburban Warriors*, 2.

21. See, for instance, Nickerson, *Mothers of Conservatism*.

22. Hemmer, *Messengers of the Right*, 76.

23. Major, "Conservative Consciousness and the Press."

24. New Hampshire wasn't the first state to pick presidential delegates in 1916; Indiana held its primary a week earlier. Four years later, New Hampshire went first.

25. Moore and Smith, *First Primary*, 13–15.

26. Sprague, "The New Hampshire Primary."

27. Moore and Smith, *First Primary*, 9.

28. Starting in 1954, voter lists printed in Nevada newspapers included both William's and Nackey's names.

29. Veblen, *The Manchester "Union Leader."*

30. Helen Kirkpatrick Milbank, "New Hampshire's Paper Tiger," *Columbia Journalism Review*, Spring 1966.

31. Wolfgang Saxon, "William Loeb Is Dead at 75; Owned Conservative Papers," *New York Times*, September 14, 1981.

32. Jane Harrigan, "Out Front," *UNH Magazine*, Spring 2011.

33. Walter V. Robinson, "Bush Honors an Old Foe—Loeb," *Boston Globe*, December 12, 1985.

34. "Around the Town," *Nashua Telegraph*, July 15, 1954.

35. Blanchard, "William Loeb"; John Morton, telephone interview with the author, February 18, 2019.

36. Helen Kirkpatrick Milbank, "New Hampshire's Paper Tiger," *Columbia Journalism Review*, Spring 1966.

37. "U.S. Appeals Court Finds for Gazette," *Boston Globe*, December 3, 1960; Helen Kirkpatrick Milbank, "New Hampshire's Paper Tiger," *Columbia Journalism Review*, Spring 1966.

38. Gfroerer, *NHPBS Presents: Powerful as the Truth*; Helen Kirkpatrick Milbank, "New Hampshire's Paper Tiger," *Columbia Journalism Review*, Spring 1966.

39. Nackey Scripps Loeb, "William Loeb, 1905–1981," *Union Leader*, September 13, 1984.

40. Joe Heaney, "Nackey Knows Challenge," *Boston Herald American*, December 6, 1981.

41. Anderson, *Little Rock*, 15.

42. William Loeb, "Paratroops, Bayonets—A Dictator's Answer," *Union Leader*, September 25, 1957.

43. Anderson, *Little Rock*, 13–15.

44. Anderson, *Little Rock*, 256; Robert Elfstrom, photo of "Brotherhood by Bayonet" bumper sticker attached to a door inside city hall in Greenwood, Missis-

sippi, in 1964, https://www.gettyimages.com.au/detail/news-photo/view-of-a
-brotherhood-of-the-bayonet-bumper-sticker-on-a-news-photo/637474466.

45. Fitch, "Citizen," 413–17.

46. Tom Muller, "Yankee Publisher Friend to South," *The Citizen*, December 1972.
(The main article was written by an assistant city editor at the *Union Leader*
for publication in *Editor & Publisher*.)

47. Nackey Scripps Loeb to George Shannon, Jackson MS, November 1, 1983, ULC.

48. Bedingfield, *Newspaper Wars*, 187.

49. Helen Kirkpatrick Milbank, "New Hampshire's Paper Tiger," *Columbia Journalism Review*, Spring 1966.

50. Moore and Smith, *First Primary*, 63–68.

51. "Washington Sunday Journal," C-SPAN, February 18, 1996; Nackey Scripps
Loeb, "The 1988 Primary: Look Before You Leap," *Union Leader*, January 26,
1987.

52. Nackey Scripps Loeb, "The 1988 Primary: Look Before You Leap," *Union Leader*,
January 26, 1987.

53. Carl Bernstein and Bob Woodward, "FBI Finds Nixon Aides Sabotaged Democrats," *Washington Post*, October 10, 1972.

54. Moore and Smith, *First Primary*, 76–78; "Jane Muskie, Senator's Wife, Dies at
77," *New York Times*, December 29, 2004.

55. "New Hampshire Primary and Dupont Endorsement," C-SPAN, February 12,
1988.

56. Pat Buchanan, interview with the author, McClean VA, August 8, 2018.

4. SURVIVING FOR A REASON

1. "Nackey Loeb Sues Nevada Auto Firm," *Burlington Daily News*, July 7, 1978.
Nackey sued the car dealership that had put new snow tires on the Jeep two
days before the accident, claiming that one of the wheels wasn't attached properly. The case was later settled out of court, with the dealership awarding Loeb
$800,000.

2. "Loeb, Wife Injured in Crash as Car Skids in Nevada," *Boston Globe*, December 19, 1977; "Publisher's Wife Critical after Reno Auto Accident," December
19, 1977; "Mrs. Loeb Paralyzed after Nevada Crash," *Boston Globe*, December
21, 1977; "Loeb Reviews Accident; Wife Injured Seriously," *Nashua Telegraph*,
December 23, 1977; "Publisher's Wife Home, but Remains Paralyzed," *Orlando
Sentinel*, April 20, 1978.

3. Photo of Nackey Scripps Loeb returning to Boston after accident, January 6,
1978, box 1015936232, "Loeb, William," BGLC; Nackey Scagliotti, email interview

with the author, January 2019; Mary Baures, "Nackey Loeb Triumph Over Tragedy," *New Hampshire Profiles*, September/October 1991.

4. Nackey Scagliotti, email interview with the author.

5. Joe Heaney, "Nackey Knows Challenge," *Boston Herald American*, December 6, 1981.

6. Wolfgang Saxon, "William Loeb Is Dead at 75; Owned Conservative Papers," *New York Times*, September 14, 1981.

7. Nackey Scripps Loeb to Clayton Brown, July 20, 1993, ULC.

8. Mary Baures, "Nackey Loeb Triumph Over Tragedy," *New Hampshire Profiles*, September/October 1991.

9. Baures, "Positive Transformations."

10. Ann Marie Williams, "There Is Nothing So Powerful as Nackey S. Loeb," *New Hampshire Business Digest*, June 1985.

11. Joe Heaney, "Nackey Knows Challenge," *Boston Herald American*, December 6, 1981.

12. Gfroerer, *NHPBS Presents: Powerful as the Truth*; Mary Baures, "Nackey Loeb Triumph Over Tragedy," *New Hampshire Profiles*, September/October 1991.

13. "Brunch and Politics in New Hampshire," C-SPAN, February 16, 1992.

14. Elisabeth Bumiller, "Following the Leader; Publisher Nackey Loeb Standing Guard on the Democrats," *Washington Post*, February 25, 1984.

15. Elisabeth Bumiller, "Following the Leader; Publisher Nackey Loeb Standing Guard on the Democrats," *Washington Post*, February 25, 1984.

16. Union Leader Corporation, internal memo, October 28, 1986, ULC.

17. Joe McQuaid to Jerome H. Walker Jr. (managing editor of *Editor & Publisher*), New York, August 17, 1983, ULC.

18. "The Loeb Legacy," *Columbia Journalism Review*, Fall 1983, 14–15.

19. Joe McQuaid, interview with the author at the *Union Leader* offices, December 20, 2018.

20. Internal Union Leader Corporation, memos, September 4, 1985, ULC.

21. Tom Thibeault, telephone interview with the author, February 4, 2019.

22. Brad Pokorny, "At the Union Leader, Has the Loeb Style Mellowed?," *Boston Globe*, April 18, 1982.

23. Nackey Scripps Loeb, "The Race for Governor, and Where We Stand," *Union Leader*, April 12, 1982.

24. Nackey Scripps Loeb, "The Dealer Takes All," *Union Leader*, August 3, 1982.

25. Robert Turner, "Mrs. Loeb Maintains Union Leader's Clout," *Boston Globe*, February 3, 1983.

26. Nackey Scripps Loeb, "Little Doug's Ferret," *Union Leader*, May 29, 1983; J. W. McQuaid, "Nackey Loeb: William Loeb's Widow Wields Her Influence," *Editor &*

Publisher, August 27, 1983; "Summary of State- and Territory-Level Ferret Regulations," American Ferret Association, Inc., ferret.org (accessed February 19, 2019).

27. Joe McQuaid to Jerome H. Walker Jr. (managing editor of *Editor & Publisher*), New York, August 17, 1983, ULC.

28. Christopher Marquis, "Meldrim Thomson, 89, Dies; Governed New Hampshire," *New York Times*, April 20, 2001.

29. Meldrim Thomson Jr, "The First Lady of New Hampshire: Nackey Scripps Loeb," *Conservative Digest*, February 1987.

30. "Washington Sunday Journal," C-SPAN, February 18, 1996.

31. Nackey Scripps Loeb to Massachusetts Rifle Association, October 5, 1983, ULC.

32. Edith and her family eventually moved to a different home. Nackey received help from a mix of family members and paid caregivers.

33. Nackey Scagliotti, email interview with the author, January 2019.

34. Nackey Scripps Loeb to Joseph Elia, Reno, December 18, 1986, ULC.

35. Nackey Scripps Loeb to Bob Scripps, January 11, 1983, ULC.

36. Nackey Scripps Loeb to staff of Nevada Star Ranch, June 15, 1983; Nackey Scripps Loeb to Joseph Elia, Reno, May 12, 1987, ULC.

37. Nackey Scripps Loeb to Nellie Allen, July 24, 1989, ULC.

38. Nackey Scagliotti, email interview with the author, January 2019.

39. Nackey Scripps Loeb to James W. Hendrick, Oklahoma City, February 6, 1989; Nackey Scagliotti, email interview with the author, January 2019.

40. Susan McLean Owen obituary, *Pasadena Star-News*, December 31, 2008; Nackey Scagliotti, email interview with the author, January 2019.

41. Nackey Scripps Loeb to Bob Scripps, January 25, 1983, ULC.

42. John Clayton, telephone interview with the author, February 20, 2019.

43. David Shribman, "Eccentric Editor Wooed at Election Time," *Wall Street Journal*, reprinted in *Globe and Mail* (Canada), September 14, 1987.

44. Nackey Scripps Loeb to Joseph Elia, Reno, January 2, 1986, and January 3, 1986, ULC.

45. "'Cripple' Is Not a Dirty Word Mrs. Loeb Tells Handicapped," *Union Leader*, October 3, 1983.

46. Nackey Scripps Loeb, "Hire the Handicapped," *Union Leader*, October 21, 1986.

47. Nackey Scripps Loeb, "Hire the Handicapped," *Union Leader*, October 5, 1987.

48. Union Leader Corporation, internal memo, August 27, 1986, ULC.

49. William F. Buckley, "On Eye-Opening," Universal Press Syndicate, August 11, 1987.

50. Nackey Scripps Loeb, "Buckley Ran Aground," *Union Leader*, August 31, 1987.

51. Nackey Scripps Loeb to Ronald Reagan, Washington DC, Mary 29, 1984, ULC.

52. Nackey Scripps Loeb to Patrick Buchanan, April 24, 1984, PBP.

53. Nackey Scripps Loeb, "Bad Bill for the Disabled," *Union Leader*, September 12, 1989.

54. "A Political Profile of Disabled Americans," Pew Research Center, September 22, 2016.

55. Ari Ne'eman, "Disability Politics Liberals, Conservatives, and the Disability-Rights Movement," *New Atlantis*, Spring 2009. There are, however, some areas where issues important to the disability rights movement do overlap with conservatism, such as opposition to selective abortion, euthanasia, and some matters of bioethics.

56. Nackey Scripps Loeb, "Bad Bill for the Disabled," *Union Leader*, September 12, 1989.

5. NEEDLE, NOT SWORD

1. Nackey Scripps Loeb, "Chicken Veep's Veep," *Union Leader*, July 15, 1984.

2. Nackey Scripps Loeb, "This 'Gerry' Thinks the Voters Are Jerks," *Union Leader*, August 14, 1984.

3. Nackey Scripps Loeb, "Chicken Veep's Veep," *Union Leader*, July 15, 1984.

4. Aday and Devitt, "Style over Substance."

5. Shawne K. Wickham, "Publisher Attacks Credentials," *Union Leader*, July 13, 1984.

6. Nickerson, *Mothers of Conservatism*, 170.

7. For instance, McRae, *Mothers of Massive Resistance*.

8. Rymph, *Republican Women*, 2.

9. Eleanor Blau, "Women's GOP Club Honors Foe of the ERA," *New York Times*, April 17, 1977; UPI photo of Nackey and William Loeb at the 1977 Women's National Republican Club luncheon, April 16, 1977, box 1015936232, BGLC.

10. Critchlow, *Phyllis Schlafly*, 151.

11. Heckman, "Needle, Not Sword."

12. Nackey Scripps Loeb to William Burleigh, June 4, 1990, ULC.

13. Heckman, "Needle, Not Sword."

14. Nackey Scripps Loeb to Joseph Wershba, November 29, 1983, ULC.

15. Nackey Scripps Loeb to George Rogers, September 20, 1983, ULC.

16. "Union Leader," C-SPAN, February 21, 1984.

17. Nackey Scripps Loeb, "Hollywood Hugh's Makeup Is Beginning to Crack," *Union Leader*, April 14, 1982.

18. For instance, Nackey Scripps Loeb, "Cleaning Up Our Own Front Yards," *Union Leader*, October 16, 1989; Nackey Scripps Loeb, "A Wakeup Call," *Union Leader*, April 23, 1993.

19. Nackey Scripps Loeb, "Ling, Ling's Fling, Fling," *Union Leader*, August 19, 1986.

20. Heckman, "Needle, Not Sword"; Gfroerer, NHPBS *Presents: Powerful as the Truth*.

21. Nackey Scripps Loeb, "'Rocky' and Social Value," *Union Leader*, November 16, 1983.

22. Nackey Scripps Loeb, "The Cheated Generation," *Union Leader*, March 24, 1987.

23. Nackey Scripps Loeb, "An Open Letter to Teenagers," *Union Leader*, April 7, 1983.

24. Nackey Scripps Loeb, "We're Asking Teens Why They Quit School," *Union Leader*, August 12, 1986.

25. Nackey Scripps Loeb, "Skateboards," *Union Leader*, July 30, 1988.

26. Nackey Scripps Loeb, "The Great NH Cat Contest," *Union Leader*, July 12, 1983.

27. Nackey Scripps Loeb, "Be Our Valentine," *Union Leader*, February 14, 1985.

28. Nackey Scripps Loeb, "Happy Birthday, Mr. President," *Union Leader*, February 6, 1987.

29. "The Loeb Legacy," *Columbia Journalism Review*, Fall 1983, 14–15.

30. Joseph Wershba to Nackey Scripps Loeb, June 20, 1983, ULC.

31. Joseph Wershba to Nackey Scripps Loeb, February 15, 1983, ULC.

32. Joseph Wershba to Nackey Scripps Loeb, August 6, 1987, ULC.

33. Sohn, "Women in Newspaper Management." It's unclear how many of those management jobs included publishing responsibilities. The first widespread gender census of U.S. newsrooms didn't happen until the late 1990s; the count cited here was performed by journalist Dorothy Jurney using the *Editor & Publisher Directory*. For more on this and other early efforts to diversify journalism, see Mellinger, *Chasing Newsroom Diversity*.

34. Joe Strupp, "Breaking Through," *MediaWeek*, November 3, 2003.

35. Byline count performed by author, January 2019, using information available on pulitzer.org.

36. Harp, Bachmann, and Loke, "Where Are the Women?"

37. Women's Media Center, *Women in the U.S. Media*.

38. Women's Media Center, *Women in the U.S. Media*.

39. Nackey Scripps Loeb, "To the Ladies of N.H. She Said It All!," *Union Leader*, January 24, 1975.

40. Nackey Scripps Loeb, "Domestic Violence: Take It Seriously," *Union Leader*, October 4, 1988.

41. Nackey Scripps Loeb, "The ERA, May It RIP," *Union Leader*, November 21, 1983.

42. Nackey Scripps Loeb, "What Women's Issues," *Union Leader*, August 3, 1988.

43. Nackey Scripps Loeb, "I Am an Angry Woman," *Union Leader*, January 25, 1993.

44. Union Leader Corporation, internal memo, February 8, 1991, ULC.

45. Heckman, "Needle, Not Sword."

46. Nackey Scripps Loeb, "Here's Your Chance," *Union Leader*, November 7, 1985.

47. Nackey Scripps Loeb, "New Hampshire Has Spoken," *Union Leader*, August 7, 1989.

48. Nackey Scripps Loeb, "They're After Our Guns Again," *Union Leader*, January 8, 1990.

49. Nackey Scripps Loeb, "On the King Holiday: Not NH Guilt Complex," *Union Leader*, January 21, 1986.

50. For instance, Kristine Phillips, "In the Latest JFK Files: The FBI's Ugly Analysis on Martin Luther King, Jr., Filled with Falsehoods," *Washington Post*, November 4, 2017.

51. "Communism," *Martin Luther King, Jr. Encyclopedia*, Martin Luther King, Jr. Research and Education Institute, Stanford University, https://kinginstitute .stanford.edu/encyclopedia/communism.

52. Michael Brindley, "N.H.'s Martin Luther King Jr. Day Didn't Happen without A Fight," New Hampshire Public Radio, August 27, 2013, NHPR.org.

53. Abraham McLaughlin, "Granite State Struggles with Civil Rights on Civil Rights Day," *Christian Science Monitor*, January 16, 1996.

54. Nackey Scripps Loeb, "White Supremacists Need Not Apply in NH," *Union Leader*, January 11, 1996.

6. A PERSONAL CONNECTION

1. Matthew L. Wald, "Boston Globe Target: New Hampshire," *New York Times*, June 7, 1987.

2. Nackey Scripps Loeb to Ronald Reagan, March 31, 1987, ULC.

3. Nackey Scripps Loeb, "What Now? Bill Loeb Will Live Because the Union Leader Will Live," *Union Leader*, September 15, 1981.

4. "New Hampshire Primary and Pete DuPont Endorsement," C-SPAN, February 13, 1988.

5. Matthew L. Wald, "Boston Globe Target: New Hampshire," *New York Times*, June 7, 1987; U.S. Census Bureau, census.gov. New Hampshire's population in 1980 was roughly 930,000. By 1990 it had grown to 1.1 million.

6. "WMUR: Who we are and where we came from," June 9, 2016, https://www .wmur.com/article/wmur-past-present-and-future/5138598.

7. One thing Nackey didn't have to worry about, at least not a first, was cable news. Although it was growing in popularity during the 1980s, many of New Hampshire's rural towns wouldn't have the option to connect until the 1990s.

8. Joe McQuaid, interview with the author at the *Union Leader* offices, December 22, 2018.

9. Union Leader Corporation, internal memos, May 24, 1983; October 27, 1986; October 28, 1986; and February 6, 1987, ULC.

10. The *Union Leader* grew just under 1 percent daily and 3 percent Sunday between 1981 and 1986, compared to flat daily growth and 1.3 percent Sunday growth nationally during the same time.

11. Union Leader Corporation, internal memos, October 27, 1986; October 28, 1986; February 6, 1987, and September 2, 1988, ULC.

12. Union Leader Corporation, internal memo, March 20, 1986, ULC. The paper also subscribed to multiple wire services, including UPI and the Associated Press, which employed a total of nine journalists assigned to cover New Hampshire.

13. Ken Doctor, "The Halving of America's Daily Newsrooms," *Nieman Lab*, July 28, 2015.

14. Tom Fahey, telephone interview with the author, March 13, 2019.

15. Dirk Ruemenapp, telephone interview with the author, March 13, 2019.

16. Union Leader Corporation, internal memo, February 12, 1988, ULC.

17. Union Leader Corporation, internal memo, June 1, 1987, ULC.

18. Tom Thibeault, telephone interview with the author, February 4, 2019.

19. Tom Thibeault, telephone interview with the author, February 4, 2019.

20. Nackey Scripps Loeb to Jim Scripps, August 13, 1982, ULC.

21. Union Leader Corporation, internal memo, February 9, 1987, ULC.

22. John Morton, telephone interview with the author, February 18, 2019.

23. Nackey Scripps Loeb to Joseph Elia, Reno, November 27, 1987; Union Leader Corporation, internal memo, February 27, 1984, ULC.

24. Robert Slimp to Nackey Scripps Loeb, July 7, 1988, ULC.

25. Edward Fike to Nackey Scripps Loeb, April 17, 1987; Nackey Scripps Loeb to Edward Fike, August 4, 1987, ULC.

26. Nackey Scripps Loeb to Jesse Helms, March 12, 1987, ULC. Nackey wrote, "I have always been an admirer of you and the work you are doing. We seem to agree with each other on many points."

27. Jesse Helms to Nackey Scripps Loeb, March 17, 1987, ULC.

28. Greg Sullivan, telephone interview with the author, February 28, 2019. The cases are *Union Leader Corp v. City of Nashua* and *Union Leader Corp v. New Hampshire Housing Finance Authority*.

29. Nackey Scripps Loeb, "Liberal Media Back to Old Tricks," *Union Leader*, November 22, 1994.

30. Nackey Scripps Loeb, "Blatant Media Bias," *Union Leader*, February 1, 1983.

31. Nackey Scripps Loeb, "White House Invite to Tutu Was Foolish," *Union Leader*, December 8, 1984.

32. Nackey Scripps Loeb, "Character Counts," *Union Leader*, September 18, 1996.

33. Nackey Scripps Loeb to Joseph Elia, Reno, August 8, 1989, ULC.

34. Nackey Scripps Loeb to Mel and Gale Thomson, December 2, 1988, ULC.

35. Nackey Scripps Loeb to Clayton Brown, December 18, 1986, ULC.

36. Nackey Scripps Loeb to Ronald Reagan, March 24, 1987, ULC.

37. Nackey Scripps Loeb, "Is Olive North a Hero?," *Union Leader*, Friday July 17, 1987.

38. Nackey Scripps Loeb, "Write!," *Union Leader*, July 14, 1987.

39. Union Leader Corporation, internal memos, May 16, 1989, and May 23, 1989, ULC.

40. Oliver North to Nackey Scripps Loeb, Manchester NH, June 2, 1989, ULC.

41. For more on how moving away from downtown harmed local newspapers, see Kennedy, *Wired City*.

42. Nackey Scripps Loeb to Clayton Brown, November 21, 1989, ULC.

43. Nackey Scripps Loeb to John Morton, April 13, 1990, ULC.

44. Nackey Scripps Loeb to Clayton Brown, May 29, 1989; Nackey Scripps Loeb to Joseph Elia, Reno, June 13, 1989, ULC.

45. Glenn Wallace, "The Union Leader Publishes on the Run for Three Days," *Union Leader*, August 27, 1990.

46. Nackey Scripps Loeb to Joseph Elia, August 26, 1990, ULC.

47. Nackey Scripps Loeb to Joseph Elia, Reno, November 16, 1990, ULC.

48. Union Leader Corporation, internal memo, February 9, 1987, ULC.

49. Union Leader Corporation, internal memo, February 9, 1987, ULC.

50. Union Leader Corporation, internal memo, June 18, 1990, ULC.

51. Nackey Scripps Loeb to Oliver North, July 31, 1990, ULC.

52. "Union Leader," C-SPAN, February 24, 1984.

53. Roy McDonald (publisher of the *Chattanooga News-Free Press*) to Nackey Scripps Loeb, November 24, 1984, ULC.

54. "Newspaper Pulls Parade Magazine," UPI, October 27, 1984.

55. Union Leader Corporation, internal memo, May 3, 1988, ULC; Laurinda Keys, "South African Miners, Mostly Blacks, Endure Heat, Danger Digging for Gold," *New Hampshire Sunday News*, May 1, 1988.

56. For instance, Nackey Scripps Loeb, "Perverse Power," *Union Leader*, November 4, 1987, and "Big Brother and Your Church," *Union Leader*, September 6, 1989.

57. Nackey Scripps Loeb, "Comic Propaganda," *Union Leader*, March 26, 1993.

58. Laura Kiernan, "For Better but Not Necessarily for Worse," *Boston Globe*, March 27, 1993.

59. Assorted letters to the editor, April 1993, ULC.
60. Nackey Scripps Loeb to multiple readers, April 1993, ULC.

7. DEAR MRS. LOEB

1. Nackey Scripps Loeb, "A New Year's Message," *Union Leader*, December 31, 1992.
2. Nackey Scripps Loeb, "Why the Union Leader Runs All Those Letters," *Union Leader*, April 30, 1982.
3. "New Hampshire Primary and DuPont Endorsement," C-SPAN, February 13, 1988.
4. For more on this phenomenon among far-right activists in the 1970s, 1980s, and early 1990s, see Belew, *Bring the War Home*; for an account of similar publications, including the rise of viral emails, in more recent decades, see Neiwert, *Alt-America*.
5. McPherson, *Conservative Resurgence*, 135.
6. For instance, William Loeb to Joseph Wershba, April 8, 1980, JSW.
7. Matthew Lancombe, "Trump Is at the NRA Today: It Didn't Used to Be a Republican Ally," *Washington Post*, April 26, 2019.
8. For instance, Nackey Scripps Loeb to Elizabeth Copeland, Roswell GA, March 27, 1987, ULC.
9. Union Leader Corporation, internal memo, n.d., ULC.
10. Clayton Brown, "The Georgia Experience," *Union Leader*, April 8, 1987.
11. Nackey Scripps Loeb to Ann Neamon, McLean VA, January 11, 1983, ULC.
12. Barbara Carton, "Helping Secure 'The Moral Order of the World,'" *Washington Post*, November 22, 1984.
13. "Biased Reporting of Library of Congress on School Prayers," October 1980, part 2, box C-88, folder 671, HHC; Anne Neamon to Nackey Scripps Loeb, August 16, 1983, and February 18, 1983, ULC.
14. Union Leader Corporation, internal memo, n.d., ULC.
15. Americans for Sane Policies, newsletter, January 1991, issue 171, Part 11, box D-13, folder 15A:133, HHC.
16. Alyn Denham to Nackey Scripps Loeb, March 17, 1987, ULC.
17. Nackey Scripps Loeb to Chuck Douglas, March 21, 1989, ULC.
18. Nackey Scripps Loeb to Alyn Denham, September 9, 1987, ULC.
19. Clint Roswell, "Simon Sweeps Endorsement; Dems Favored in 7 Council Races," *Daily News* (New York), November 3, 1985.
20. Union Leader Corporation, internal memo, n.d., ULC.
21. Nackey Scripps Loeb to Michael Barrow, October 19, 1987, ULC.
22. Thomas P. Ronan, "Wallace to Run in Primary Here," *New York Times*, November 21, 1975.

23. Mark Bablin to Nackey Scripps Loeb, May 26, 1988, ULC.

24. For instance, Nackey Scripps Loeb to Alyn Denham, April 24, 1986, ULC.

25. For instance, Nackey Scripps Loeb to Michael Barrow, September 29, 1987, ULC. Enclosures included five copies of an editorial.

26. Nackey Scripps Loeb to Alyn Denham, March 2, 1987, ULC.

27. Nackey Scripps Loeb to Bob Smith, December 23, 1986, ULC.

28. Clifford Krauss, "Senators Divided on M.I.A. Survival," *New York Times*, January 13, 1993.

29. Nildo Harper, "U.S. Post Office Celebrates 'Pride Day,'" *Lambda Philatelic Journal*, Summer 1989.

30. U.S. Sen. Gordon Humphrey to Postmaster General Anthony M. Frank, June 30, 1989, ULC.

31. Nackey Scripps Loeb, "Our Government Promotes Sodomy," *Union Leader*, July 5, 1989.

32. Nackey Scripps Loeb, "I Think We Are in a Helluva Mess," *Union Leader*, April 8, 1987.

33. Nackey Scripps Loeb, "Warning from Georgia," *Union Leader*, September 27, 1989.

34. Nackey Scripps Loeb, "A Perilous Time," *Union Leader*, December 6, 1984.

35. Nackey Scripps Loeb, "Labor Day, Labor Unions," *Union Leader*, September 1, 1986. Both Nackey and Denham stressed that they valued the contributions organized labor had made in terms of worker safety and fair wages but disliked the way many unions had become involved in politics; Nackey Scripps Loeb, "It All Depends Who Is President," *Union Leader*, May 28, 1987.

36. Marra for President campaign flyer, n.d., ULC.

37. Michael Barrow to Nackey Scripps Loeb, December 13, 1987, ULC.

38. Nackey Scripps Loeb to Michael Barrow, December 17, 1987, ULC.

39. Nackey Scripps Loeb, "Democrats Have Choice with Dr. Marra," *Union Leader*, February 6, 1988.

40. After dropping out of the Democratic race, Marra went on to run as the Right to Life Party's 1988 nominee.

41. Michael Barrow to Nackey Scripps Loeb, March 23, 1988, ULC.

42. Union Leader Corporation, internal memo, November 24, 1986, ULC.

43. Nackey Scripps Loeb to Alyn Denham, February 2, 1990, ULC. In late 1990 Denham announced he would stop publishing his newsletter the following year.

44. Mark Bablin to Nackey Scripps Loeb, November 8, 1987, ULC.

45. Clayton Brown to Nackey Scripps Loeb, December 4, 1987, ULC.

46. Nackey Scripps Loeb to Alyn Denham, April 28, 1987, ULC.

47. Meg Heckman, "When Reluctant Presidential Candidates Need a Push," *Boston Globe*, March 6, 2015; Moore and Smith, *First Primary*, 50–52 and 239.

48. Nackey Scripps Loeb, "Presidential Race: It's Not Too Late," *Union Leader*, September 2, 1987.

49. Nackey Scripps Loeb, "Jeane Kirkpatrick Welcome to New Hampshire," *Union Leader*, September 25, 1987.

50. Tim Weiner, "Jeane Kirkpatrick, Reagan's Forceful Envoy, Dies," *New York Times*, December 9, 2006.

51. Clayton Brown to Nackey Scripps Loeb, May 30, 1987, ULC.

52. Thomas B. Edsall, "Kirkpatrick Quiets Speculation on Candidacy," *Washington Post*, September 26, 1987. Fike's pro-Kirkpatrick column was quoted widely in the political press, including this *Washington Post* article.

53. Nackey Scripps Loeb to Jeane Kirkpatrick, April 21, 1987, ULC.

54. Nackey Scripps Loeb to Jeane Kirkpatrick, March 20, 1987, ULC.

55. Nackey Scripps Loeb to Jeane Kirkpatrick, August 10, 1987, ULC.

56. Jeane Kirkpatrick to Nackey Scripps Loeb, April 3, 1987, ULC.

57. Nackey Scripps Loeb to Jeane Kirkpatrick, April 21, 1987, ULC.

58. Union Leader Corporation, internal memo, September 2, 1987; Nackey Scripps Loeb to Edward Fike, September 29, 1987, ULC.

59. Nackey Scripps Loeb to Joseph Elia, September 14, 1987, ULC.

60. Jeane Kirkpatrick to Nackey Scripps Loeb, November 20, 1987, ULC.

61. Nackey Scripps Loeb to Jeane Kirkpatrick, November 3, 1987, ULC.

62. Nackey Scripps Loeb to Edward Fike, November 24, 1987, ULC.

8. THE "WIMP" IN WASHINGTON

1. Nackey Scripps Loeb, "The 1988 Primary: Look Before You Leap," *Union Leader*, January 26, 1987.

2. "Kemp Featured Speaker at Dinner for Mrs. Loeb," *Union Leader*, April 12, 1984.

3. Nackey Scripps Loeb to Patrick Buchanan, February 24, 1987, ULC.

4. Michael Birkner, "The Big What-If of the GOP Race in '88," *Concord Monitor*, January 23, 1988.

5. Nackey Scripps Loeb, "Why Vote for Bob Dole?," *Union Leader*, January 22, 1988.

6. Nackey Scripps Loeb, "Whither Now, Conservative Voters?," *Union Leader*, February 4, 1988.

7. Nackey Scripps Loeb, "Whither Now, Conservative Voters?," *Union Leader*, February 4, 1988.

8. Gerald M. Boyd, "The Paradox of Pete DuPont: Political Iconoclast with Establishment Roots," *New York Times*, December 28, 1987.

9. Moore and Smith, *First Primary*, 95–100.

10. Nackey Scripps Loeb, "None of the Above," *Union Leader*, April 21, 1988.

11. Nackey Scripps Loeb, "What Bush Must Do," *Union Leader*, June 8, 1988.

12. Nackey Scripps Loeb, "What Bush Must Do," *Union Leader*, June 8, 1988.

13. Nackey Scripps Loeb, "Child Danger: Politics Ahead," *Union Leader*, August 2, 1988.

14. Nackey Scripps Loeb, "Dukakis and Abortion," *Union Leader*, October 19, 1988.

15. Nackey Scripps Loeb, "An Amazing Campaign," *Union Leader*, October 31, 1988.

16. Nackey Scripps Loeb, "An Amazing Campaign," *Union Leader*, October 31, 1988.

17. "Kitty Dukakis Flag Rumor Is Rebutted," *Indianapolis Star*, August 25, 1988; "Senator Backs Off Flag-Burning Charges," *Boston Globe*, August 27, 1988.

18. Nackey Scripps Loeb to George H. W. Bush, September 16, 1988, ULC.

19. Nackey Scripps Loeb to George H. W. Bush, November 15, 1988, ULC.

20. Nackey Scripps Loeb to Alyn Denham, April 25, 1989, ULC.

21. Nackey Scripps Loeb to Mark Bablin, October 29, 1990, ULC.

22. Nackey Scripps Loeb to Joseph C. Elia, Reno, September 11, 1989, ULC.

23. Nackey Scripps Loeb, "Mr. President, What Are You Doing?," *Union Leader*, May 9, 1989.

24. Nackey Scripps Loeb, "U.S. Foreign Policy Is Bush League," *Union Leader*, October 13, 1989.

25. Nackey Scripps Loeb, "Interesting Theory on Bush and North," *Union Leader*, October 26,61989.

26. Nackey Scripps Loeb, "Mr. President, What Are You Doing?," *Union Leader*, May 9, 1989.

27. Nackey Scripps Loeb to Clayton Brown, February 23, 1990, ULC.

28. Nackey Scripps Loeb to Charles Scripps, February 2, 1990, ULC.

29. Union Leader Corporation, internal memo, n.d., ULC.

30. Union Leader Corporation, internal memo, n.d., ULC.

31. Nackey Scripps Loeb, "Backyard Picnic at the House," *Union Leader*, August 28, 1984.

32. Nackey Scripps Loeb to Joseph Elia, November 16, 1990, ULC.

33. Clayton Brown to Nackey Scripps Loeb, December 21, 1992, ULC.

34. Mark Bablin to Nackey Scripps Loeb, November 15, 1989, ULC.

35. Mark Bablin to Nackey Scripps Loeb, April 8, 1990, ULC.

36. For instance, Goldman et al., *Quest*, 297–311.

37. Goldman et al., *Quest*, 13.

38. Nackey Scripps Loeb, "Welcome Back, Pat Buchanan," *Union Leader*, March 17, 1986.

39. Nackey Scripps Loeb, "Come Again, Pat," *Union Leader*, March 19, 1986.

40. "Pat Buchanan for President?," *Human Events*, November 22, 1986, ULC.

41. Nackey Scripps Loeb to Joseph Elia, July 27, 1989, ULC.

42. Patrick Buchanan, interview with the author, McLean VA, August 8, 2018.

43. Stanley, *Crusader*, 135.

44. Patrick Buchanan to Nackey Scripps Loeb, April 6, 1990, ULC.

45. Nackey Scripps Loeb to Patrick J. Buchanan, June 18, 1990, ULC.

46. Nackey Scripps Loeb to Patrick Buchanan, July 9, 1990, ULC.

47. Patrick Buchanan, interview with the author, McLean VA, August 8, 2018.

48. Nackey Scripps Loeb to Patrick J. Buchanan, October 29, 1990, ULC.

9. POLITICAL GODMOTHER

1. Germond and Witcover, *Mad as Hell*, 130–32.

2. Nackey Scripps Loeb, "Bring on the Primary," *Union Leader*, January 16, 1991.

3. "Buchanan Speech Sounds Strong Conservative Theme," *Union Leader*, January 17, 1991.

4. Nackey Scripps Loeb to W. E. Scott, January 4, 1991, ULC.

5. Nackey Scripps Loeb, "They Protest Too Much," *Union Leader*, January 21, 1991, ULC.

6. Nackey Scripps Loeb to Bay Buchanan, January 17, 1991, ULC.

7. Nackey Scripps Loeb to Patrick Buchanan, April 21, 1991, ULC.

8. Germond and Witcover, *Mad as Hell*, 62–72, 133.

9. Nackey Scripps Loeb, "America First," *Union Leader*, September 18, 1991.

10. Goldman et al., *Quest*, 318.

11. Bay Buchanan, telephone with the author, October 5, 2018.

12. Nackey Scripps Loeb, "An NH Challenge for George Bush," *Union Leader*, November 8, 1991.

13. Nackey Scripps Loeb to Patrick Buchanan, November 8, 1991, ULC.

14. Bay Buchanan, telephone interview with the author, October 5, 2018.

15. Nackey Scripps Loeb, "Pat Buchanan for President," *Union Leader*, January 22, 1992.

16. Goldman et al., *Quest*, 319–20.

17. "A Special Olympics," *New Republic*, March 9, 1992.

18. "Is Pat Buchanan Anti-Semitic?," *Newsweek*, December 22, 1991.

19. Mike McAlary, "Hatemonger Worked While George Stood Pat," *New York Post*, undated clipping, ULC.

20. Nackey Scripps Loeb, "A Clear Choice: Cop-Out or Conviction," *Union Leader*, February 12, 1992.

21. "Brunch and Politics in New Hampshire," C-SPAN, February 16, 1992.

22. Nackey Scripps Loeb, "There's Nothing Wrong with This Negative," *Union Leader*, February 17, 1992.

23. Moore and Smith, *First Primary*, 103–9.

24. Moore and Smith, *First Primary*, 107–9.

25. "Washington Sunday Journal," C-SPAN, February 18, 1996.

26. "Washington Sunday Journal," C-SPAN, February 18, 1996.

27. "Washington Sunday Journal," C-SPAN, February 18, 1996; Nackey Scripps Loeb to Edward Fike, February 5, 1992, ULC.

28. Moore and Smith, *First Primary*, 108.

29. Nackey Scripps Loeb, "Where Pat Goes from Here," *Union Leader*, February 21, 1992.

30. Nackey Scripps Loeb, "Pat Buchanan for Vice President," *Union Leader*, July 9, 1992.

31. Nackey Scripps Loeb to Patrick Buchanan, March 25, 1992, ULC.

32. Patrick Buchanan, "1992 Republican National Convention Speech," Patrick J. Buchanan Official Website, August 17, 1992, https://buchanan.org/blog/1992-republican-national-convention-speech-148.

33. Patrick Buchanan, interview with the author, McLean VA, August 8, 2018.

34. Nackey Scagliotti, email interview with the author, January 2019.

35. Nackey Scripps Loeb to Joseph Elia, June 30, 1993, ULC.

36. Nackey Scripps Loeb to Patrick Buchanan, September 20, 1994, ULC.

37. Nackey Scripps Loeb to Patrick Buchanan, May 1, 1995, ULC.

38. "Washington Sunday Journal," C-SPAN, March 20, 1995.

39. Farnsworth and Lichter, "The Manchester Union Leader's Influence."

40. Moore and Smith, *First Primary*, 110.

41. Michael Kranish, "Buchanan Tops GOP's Big 3," *Boston Globe*, February 21, 1996.

42. Patrick Buchanan, "1996 Victory Speech—Manchester, NH," Patrick J. Buchanan Official Website, February 20, 1996, https://buchanan.org/blog/1996-victory-speech-manchester-nh-183.

43. "New Hampshire Primary," C-SPAN, February 20, 1996.

CONCLUSION

1. Nackey Scripps Loeb, "Don't Come Back, Kid," *Union Leader*, February 18, 1999.

2. David Nyhan, "Clinton in N.H.—A Lesson in Hanging Tough," *Boston Globe*, February 21, 1999.

Notes to Pages 132–141

3. Union Leader Corporation, internal memos, January 13, 1998, and January 14, 1998, ULC.

4. Union Leader Corporation, internal memos, n.d., ULC.

5. Nackey Scripps Loeb, "Stay Out of the Hot Sun," *Union Leader*, June 20, 1998.

6. Nackey Scagliotti, email interview with the author, February 2019; Greg Sullivan, telephone interview with the author, February 28, 2019.

7. The school owns 75 percent of the Union Leader Corporation. The rest is in a trust for employees.

8. Mike Retch, "Nackey Loeb Praised for Her Political Influence, Benevolence," Associated Press, January 14, 2000.

9. "New Hampshire Union Leader Retracts Christie Endorsement," CBS Boston, March 1, 2016.

10. Henry Allen, "The Iron Fist of Pat Buchanan," *Washington Post*, February 17, 1992.

Bibliography

ARCHIVES AND MANUSCRIPT MATERIALS

BGLC: Boston Globe Library Collection. M214. University Libraries, Archives and Special Collections Department, Northeastern University, Boston.

CBS: CBS News Archive. CBS, Inc., New York.

Clark, Blair. "Newspapering in New Hampshire." Unpublished manuscript, December 30, 2018.

C-SPAN: C-SPAN Video Library. https://www.c-span.org/about/videoLibrary/.

EWSC: E. W. Scripps Collection, 1868–1926. Robert E. and Jean R. Mahn Center for Archives and Special Collections, Ohio University Libraries, Athens.

Heckman, Meg. "Needle, Not Sword: How Nackey Scripps Loeb Used Editorials to Build Audiences and Influence Presidential Politics." Unpublished conference paper, Association of Educators in Journalism and Mass Communication annual conference, Washington DC, August 7, 2018.

HHC: Hall-Hoag Collection of Dissenting and Extremist Printed Propaganda. John Hay Library, Brown University, Providence, Rhode Island.

JSW: Joseph and Shirley Wershba Papers, 1936–2001. Dolph Briscoe Center for American History, University of Texas at Austin.

PBP: Selected private papers of Patrick Buchanan, McLean, Virginia.

RWH: Roy W. Howard Archive. The Media School, Indiana University, Bloomington. http://mediaschool.indiana.edu/royhowardarchive/.

ULC: Nackey Scripps Loeb Papers. Private archive, Union Leader Corporation, Manchester, New Hampshire.

VSA: Vermont State Archives. Montpelier.

PUBLISHED WORKS

Adams, Edward. "Josephine Scripps: A Modern-Day Corporate Newspaper Chain Owner: The Beginnings." *Southwestern Mass Communication Journal* 14, no. 2 (Winter 1999): 81–92.

Aday, Sean, and James Devitt. "Style over Substance: Newspaper Coverage of Elizabeth Dole's Presidential Bid." *Harvard International Journal of Press/Politics* 6, no. 2 (March 2001): 52–73.

Anderson, Karen. *Little Rock: Race and Resistance at Central High School*. Princeton NJ: Princeton University Press, 2010.

Baldasty, Gerald J. *E. W. Scripps and the Business of Newspapers*. Urbana: University of Illinois Press, 1999.

Baures, Mary Margaret. "Positive Transformations After Extreme Trauma." PhD diss., Antioch New England Graduate School, 1994. ProQuest (order no. 9523005).

Beasley, Maurine. "Recent Directions for the Study of Women's History in American Journalism." *Journalism Studies* 2, no. 2 (2001): 207–20.

Bedingfield, Sid. *Newspaper Wars: Civil Rights and White Resistance in South Carolina 1935–1965*. Urbana: University of Illinois Press, 2017.

Belew, Kathleen. *Bring the War Home: The White Power Movement and Paramilitary America*. Boston: Harvard University Press, 2018.

Blanchard, Margaret. "William Loeb." In *Dictionary of Literary Biography*. Vol. 127, *American Newspaper Publishers, 1950–1990*. Detroit: Gale Research, 1993.

Cash, Kevin. *Who the Hell Is William Loeb?* Hooksett NH: Amoskeag Press, 1975.

Casserly, Jack. *Scripps the Divided Dynasty: A History of the First Family of American Journalism*. New York: Donald I. Fine, 1993.

Critchlow, Donald T. *Phyllis Schlafly and Grassroots Conservatism: A Woman's Crusade*. Princeton; Oxford: Princeton University Press, 2005.

Everbach, Tracy. "The Culture of a Women-Led Newspaper: An Ethnographic Study of the Sarasota Herald-Tribune." *Journalism & Mass Communication Quarterly* 83, no. 3 (Autumn 2006): 477–93.

Farnsworth, Stephen J., and Robert S. Lichter. "The Manchester Union Leader's Influence in the 1996 New Hampshire Republican Primary." *Presidential Studies Quarterly* 33, no. 2 (June 2003): 291–304.

Fitch, Steven J. "Citizen 1955–1989." In *The Conservative Press in Twentieth-Century America*, edited by Ronald Lora and William Henry Longton. Westport CT: Greenwood Press, 1999.

Germond, Jack, and Jules Witcover. *Mad as Hell: Revolt at the Ballot Box, 1992*. New York: Warner Books, 1993.

Gfroerer, John, prod. NHPBS Presents: *Powerful as the Truth: William Loeb & 35 Years of NH*. Accompany, 2001.

Gillespie McRae, Elizabeth. *Mothers of Massive Resistance: White Women and the Politics of White Supremacy*. Oxford University Press, 2018.

Goldman, Peter, Thomas M. DeFrank, Mark Miller, Andrew Murr, and Tom Mathews. *Quest for the Presidency 1992*. College Station: Texas A&M University Press, 1994.

Harp, Dustin, Ingrid Bachmann, and Jamie Loke. "Where Are the Women? The Presence of Female Columnists on U.S. Opinion Pages." *Journalism and Mass Communication Quarterly* 91, no. 2 (2014): 289–307.

Hemmer, Nicole. *Messengers of the Right: Conservative Media and the Transformation of American Politics*. Philadelphia: University of Pennsylvania Press, 2016.

Kaiser, Charles. *The Gay Metropolis: The Landmark History of Gay Life in America*. New York: Grove Press, 1997.

Kennedy, Dan. *The Wired City: Reimagining Journalism and Civic Life in the Post-Newspaper Age*. Amherst and Boston: University of Massachusetts Press, 2013.

Lora, Ronald, and William Henry Longton. *The Conservative Press in Twentieth-Century America*. Westport CT: Greenwood Press, 1999.

Major, Mark. "Conservative Consciousness and the Press: The Institutional Contribution to the Idea of 'Liberal Media' in Right-Wing Discourse." *Critical Sociology* 41, no. 3 (2015): 483–91.

McClain, Molly. *Ellen Browning Scripps: New Money & American Philanthropy*. Lincoln: University of Nebraska Press, 2017.

McGirr, Lisa. *Suburban Warriors: The Origins of the New American Right*. Princeton NJ: Princeton University Press, 2001.

McPherson, James Brian. *The Conservative Resurgence and the Press: The Media's Role in the Rise of the Right*. Evanston IL: Northwestern University Press, 2008.

Mellinger, Gwyneth. *Chasing Newsroom Diversity: From Jim Crow to Affirmative Action*. Urbana: University of Illinois Press, 2013.

Moore, David W., and Andrew E. Smith. *The First Primary: New Hampshire's Outsize Role in Presidential Nominations*. Durham: University of New Hampshire Press, 2015.

Neiwert, David. *Alt-America: The Rise of the Radical Right in the Age of Trump*. Brooklyn and London: Verso, 2017.

Nickerson, Michelle M. *Mothers of Conservatism Women and the Postwar Right*. Princeton NJ: Princeton University Press, 2012.

Rymph, Catherine E. *Republican Women: Feminism and Conservatism from Suffrage through the Rise of the New Right*. Chapel Hill: University of North Carolina Press, 2006.

Sheehy, Michael. "Capitalism as a Necessary Evil: How E. W. Scripps Charted a Cautious Course toward the Left." *American Journalism* 28, no. 2 (Spring 2011): 7–21.

Skinner, Kiron K., Annelise Anderson, and Martin Anderson. *Reagan: A Life in Letters*. New York: Simon and Schuster, 2004.

Sohn, Ardyth Broadrick. "Women in Newspaper Management: An Update." *Newspaper Research Journal* 3, no. 1 (1981): 94–106.

Sprague, Stuart. "The New Hampshire Primary." *Presidential Studies Quarterly* 14, no. 1 (1984): 127–31.

Stanley, Timothy. *The Crusader: The Life and Tumultuous Times of Pat Buchanan*. New York: Thomas Dunne Books, 2012.

Tuchman, Gaye. "The Symbolic Annihilation of Women by the Mass Media." In *Hearth & Home: Images of Women in the Mass Media*, 3–38. New York: Oxford University Press, 1978.

Veblen, Eric. *The Manchester "Union Leader" in New Hampshire Elections*. Lebanon NH: University Press of New England, 1975.

Women's Media Center. *The Status of Women in the U.S. Media 2017*. Washington DC: Women's Media Center, 2017.

Index

ten, biased," 4, 41–57; women's role
in, 8–9